Amazing
Saints

By Rev. T. G. Morrow

PRINTED IN THE UNITED STATES OF AMERICA

Dedication

This book is dedicated to the Blessed Virgin Mary, the most amazing of all saints; and to C. R. on her journey to holiness.

Acknowledgment

My sincere thanks to Barbara Meng and Olga Fairfax who so carefully proofread this manuscript and recommended corrections.

4

Table of Contents

Chapter One

St. Damien of Molokai. 7

Chapter Two
St. Margaret of Cortona. 69

Chapter Three
St. Augustine of Hippo. 99

Chapter Four
Bl. Miguel Agustin Pro. 133

Chapter Five
St. Teresa of Ávila. 199

Chapter Six
St. John Vianney. 283

Chapter One

St. Damien of Molokai

(1840-1889)

Greater love than this has no man, to lay down his life for his friends (Jn 15:13). St. Damien took on the huge task of ministering to the lepers on the Hawaiian island of Molokai. The whole world responded to the sacrificial offering of his life for these outcasts by calling him a hero, and a remarkable one at that. He was indeed a hero, and more, a saint.

Background

In 1825 Fr. Alexis Bachelot, was given the assignment of being a missionary to Hawaii along with two other priests and some lay brothers. They were all members of the Congregation of the Sacred Hearts of Jesus and Mary of the Perpetual Adoration of the Most Blessed Sacrament. In 1826 the small party set sail for Hawaii.

In 1820 a large number of Protestant missionaries from New England had entered Hawaii. They had been quite successful in converting the natives, including Queen Kaahumanu. As the Sacred Hearts missionaries were on their way to the islands, American ship captains warned the Hawaiian leaders that some "Jesuits" were about to arrive to prepare for French merchants to conquer Hawaii.

Americans on the islands met with the Hawaiian leaders to urge them to reject the French, and the clergy about to arrive. When the ship arrived July 7, 1827 Queen Kaahumanu refused to allow any of the missionaries to go ashore on Oahu.

However, the next day Fr. Bachelot and company received permission through the diplomatic efforts of some South Americans, to go ashore and rest from their long voyage. Fr. Bachelot refused to be thwarted by the lies of the Americans, and began to search for property for the mission. They were able to stay in Oahu because of the effort of Francisco Paul Marin, a Spaniard who had been there since 1791 and had attained an excellent reputation.

Fr. Bachelot offered the first Mass in Hawaii July 14, 1827. The missionary party was able to stay in Oahu for a few years until their supporter, Governor Boki of Honolulu was lost in an accident at sea.

On April 2, 1831, Queen Kaahumanu called in the two remaining priests, and banished them from the country. Despite diplomatic efforts, the priests were put on a ship and sent away on December 24, 1831. The two were dropped in Southern California where they began to serve as missionaries in the San Gabriel Mission near Los Angeles.

Meanwhile another priest of the Sacred Hearts, Aresnius Walsh, arrived in Honolulu with a British passport. Even though Catholics had been persecuted up until then, Fr. Walsh was surprisingly protected by the British consul. He stayed, and began to make many converts.

When Fr. Bachelot heard about Fr. Walsh's success, he returned with another priest in 1837. They were hoping that the arrival of Fr. Walsh signaled a softening of the government toward missionaries.

They were mistaken. It took the strong diplomatic efforts of foreign representatives to even get the priests off the ship and onto the island. Seeing that things had not changed enough that they would be welcome, they both planned to leave and go to another pacific island to do their missionary work. Fr Bachelot was too ill to go right away, but his companion sailed off almost immediately.

On October 6, 1837, Father Louis Maigret arrived with another Irish priest, both of the Sacred Hearts Order. Father Maigret would later become the first bishop of Hawaii. When he saw the hostile state of affairs, which extended to himself, he determined to take Fr. Bachelot elsewhere so he could find some rest and recover from his illness.

They left Hawaii November 17, 1837. However, Fr. Bachelot's health declined rather quickly, and he died on board ship December 5. Less than two weeks later the king of Hawaii put out a law "Rejecting the Catholic Religion." Anyone discovered teaching this religion was to be arrested, fined, tortured and expelled from the country.

Many were outraged at this assault on Catholicism, and it was only a matter of time before a strong response came from France. On July 9, 1839 several French warships arrived declaring that complete liberty was to be given to Catholicism in Hawaii, all jailed Catholics be set free, a site for a Catholic church be donated, and $20,000 be given over to the main ship's captain as a guarantee that all this be carried out. The $20,000 would be returned when the French government was satisfied that the conditions were met. If the conditions were not met, "war would immediately commence..."

This had the desired effect. Religious freedom was restored everywhere in the islands, and a public Mass was offered to make clear the change in policy. Americans protested, but this died out in time.

Shortly after the French triumph over Hawaiian bigotry, Bishop Stephen Rouchouze landed in Honolulu with three priests of the Sacred Hearts. He established a number of good policies governing the mission but in time decided there was a need for some religious sisters. So, he returned to Europe to gather some volunteers.

In late 1842 ten sisters, seven priests and seven lay brothers of the Sacred Hearts Order set sail for Hawaii. There was great anticipation on the islands about the new missionaries. However, as the ship became overdue, the enthusiasm waned. Day by day hope diminished. The ship and entire crew were lost.

A new leader for the Hawaiian mission was chosen, Fr. Louis Maigret. He was consecrated bishop on October 30, 1847.

Birth in Belgium

Meanwhile on January 3, 1840 Joseph de Veuster, later to be known as Fr. Damien, had been born in Tremeloo, Belgium. He was the seventh child of eight born to Francis and Ann Catherine deVeuster. They were hard-working farmers, strong in their Catholic faith. Ann used to read the lives of the saints to the children. As a result, it was no surprise that when Joseph was five his sister Eugénie joined the Ursuline sisters. When she died six years later of typhus, her sister Pauline joined in her place.

Joseph was quiet as a boy. He liked the solitude that went with his job of shepherd on the farm.

Once while skating he fell through the ice. Unfazed, he took off one of his skates and used it to cut through the ice until he could reach a stronger section to climb up on and slide to a safe area.

When he was thirteen, Joseph stopped going to school to work full time on the farm. He showed extraordinary strength in lifting hundred pound bags of grain with ease.

Joseph also demonstrated an aptitude for the business end of the farm, so in time his father sent him back to school to study management. When the boy mentioned to his father he felt called to be a monk, his father insisted he wait a while to see if it was a true calling.

Vocation

He did wait, but at the age of 18, he announced to his family, "God is calling me. I must obey." A month later he visited his brother August, now a religious in the Sacred Hearts Fathers, having taken the name Pamphile. Young Joseph applied and after some delay, was accepted in the same Order.

They were a little disappointed at his lack of education and ill manners. He seemed to be an ignorant farm boy. So, they accepted him to be a brother. His simple tasks included cleaning, caring for the chapel, caring for the sick and assisting one of the priests.

Joseph fulfilled his duties without complaint, but he had something more in mind. When he and his brother agreed to play a kind of game translating Latin, Pamphile began to see that Joseph was learning Latin very quickly. When Pamphile mentioned this to the seminary leaders, they decided to permit Joseph to study for the priesthood. However, they added two months to his novitiate.

Joseph began to change immediately. He overcame his rough manners and pursued real politeness. He showed the ability to deal with problems creatively and effectively. And, he sought to develop a spirit of serenity. He went so far as to etch the words "silence, recollection and prayer" in his desk. He worked hard at his studies and learned well, not for the sake of learning but, as one of his professors pointed out, "to become an apostle."

It was traditional in the order to take turns praying before the Blessed Sacrament. His hour was from 2:00 to 3:00 am. He loved those hours of silent prayer, as he had loved the silent hours in the early morning darkness on the farm. And, when he finished his hour, he did not need to go back to bed since he always slept so deeply and had such good health as a result.

On October 7, 1860 took final vows in Paris, taking the new name, "Damien." One of his superiors noted that while the other seminarians often moved here and there with a good deal of distraction, Damien seemed to work with a clear purpose. He had a zeal for his vocation and was not easily distracted. And, he was driven to catch up with his peers for his lack of studies in the past.

He took on a sense of modesty, feeling honored to be in the company of young men of nobler and holier background, including his brother Pamphile. He was quite content with the rules and routines of the seminary, which reminded him of similar requirements on the farm. And, it was said Damien could "outwalk, outrun and outwork everyone in the seminary."

He was described as being five feet eight and 170 pounds of muscle. His health was excellent. According to his brother Pamphile, Damien often slept on the floor as a penance, covered with just a thin blanket.

To Hawaii

In 1863 the Sacred Hearts Order was asked to send missionaries to Hawaii to bring the faith there. The superiors chose six priests to go, among whom was Pamphile de Veuster. When Pamphile came down with Typhus, Damien offered to take his place. After some time his offer was accepted.

On March 19, 1864 Damien arrived in Hawaii after a four-and-a-half month journey by sea. He was not yet ordained a priest.

He was sent to the College of Ahiumanu to finish his studies and to study the Hawaiian language and prayers. On May 24, 1864 Damien was ordained a priest by Bishop Maigret.

In June the bishop brought Damien and another newly-ordained priest aboard a ship to travel to their new assignments. They stopped on the way at Maui where they were able to offer Mass. Damien was able to obtain a good deal of advice from the seasoned missionaries there because the ship he was to board immediately after Mass was delayed due to a fire on board.

Eventually he arrived at the district of Puna on the Big Island of Hawaii, where he was to serve. There were 350 Catholics there. He wrote home to say he thought the Hawaiians to be gentle, good people. He found out rather quickly, however, that their attitudes toward sexuality left much to be desired.

So, Damien and his fellow religious set about their work. After just eight months, the priest who served the neighboring district suffered a breakdown under the tremendous work load he had. It was decided to have them trade the two districts since Damien's health suffered no ill-effects, and his area was smaller than that of the other priest.

This new district comprised almost a quarter of the island, occupying more than one thousand square miles. The land was quite primitive as was his previous district but it contained Kohala Mountain and a snow-capped mountain known as Mauna Loa. His first six weeks were spent exploring his new territory.

As he had done in Puna, he began building all sorts of structures, including eight chapels. He would go up on the mountain to cut down a large tree for the project and carry it down the hill all by himself.

The people kept bees to provide him with honey and candles for the altar. He grew tobacco, potatoes and coffee, and bred chickens, pigs and sheep.

Each Sunday the people would come to Mass in one of the chapels, the start of which was signaled by the blowing of a conch shell. Following Mass a meal was held. After that the shell was again blown to invite all to gather for the rosary and other prayers. Virtually the whole Sunday was spent in prayer, worship and a parish meal.

There was quite a competition between the different religions on the island, and Damien was ready for the challenge. When a Protestant minister was hailed for having climbed the 2000 foot cliff of Mount Kohala in just two hours, Damien went out and climbed it in forty-five minutes.

One of the drawbacks of his mission was that he had to travel 150 miles to go to confession. After some time he would be given an assistant to alleviate that problem. He seldom saw his bishop. Damien would visit Honolulu every two years to seek supplies.

Once when Bishop Maigret did visit Damien's district, he planned to bless the people and move on. However, they explained to him that such a quick visit would not do. They had to send runners to all the different villages announcing the great celebration with the bishop. When they all arrived, a great feast was held, with all sorts of delicious food.

Damien was delighted not only to have his bishop visit, but also to have someone with great experience to guide him in his mission. Of course, he was happy as well to spend time with the bishop who ordained him, and who was so vital to the Church in Hawaii.

In 1869 another priest was sent to the Big Island, Father Gulstan Ropert. He was to serve in nearby Hamakua. Damien was happy to have such a devout, humble priest whom he could visit from time to time, and to whom he could confess his sins. Fr. Gulstan would become the bishop in Hawaii 23 years later.

Damien went through times of depression in this assignment. He was deeply saddened by the frequent drunken orgies of the natives.

Distant Village

When he was told there was a remote village with some Catholics living there, he wanted to go to visit it. However, it was surrounded by high mountains and required traveling by boat just to get to the mountains. He was advised to wait several months until after the rainy season. He decided he could not wait, thinking that it was important to bring these people the sacraments. He should have waited.

He started out traveling in a canoe which capsized when they were a good distance from land. His two traveling companions wanted to swim ashore, but Damien convinced them to stay with the canoe, knowing that there were sharks in the waters. Soon enough the sharks began to circle the boat with its three ousted occupants clinging to the overturned boat for dear life. They kept splashing the water with the oars and yelling and screaming to keep the sharks away. Finally they reached the shore, happy to be safe again.

Damien decided to start over in a week. He chose to travel by way of the mountains this next time.

He began on horseback, but in a short time he had to give up the horse, as the terrain was too rough for it. He continued on foot, and soon had to swim to get to the first mountain. He climbed that steep mountain on his hands and knees as the heavy rain began to fall.

He made it to the top and saw no sign of a village, but only another high mountain beyond a ravine which lay open beneath him. He carefully let himself down the first mountain and climbed up the second. At the top he found no sign of humanity, but only a flat stretch of land followed by another hill. By this point he was covered with scratches on his hands and face and he was missing three fingernails from the rugged climb amid the rain showers.

He saw no sign of life, no animals or birds. After some more arduous climbing he reached the third peak, but again, there was no sign of humanity. Down he went and ultimately down went his body, totally exhausted and suffering from loss of blood due to his many wounds. He crumbled down unconscious.

After four days of this ordeal he had actually drawn close to the outpost he sought, and providentially, he was discovered by the villagers and brought to safety. Once they washed him, gave him some nourishment and attended to his wounds, he revived. The next day he was able to function, although he was still quite stiff from his ordeal. Nonetheless, he began to minister to the people, baptizing a child near death and preparing for Mass the next day. Following that he began to catechize the villagers and perform the sacraments.

He urged them to build a chapel and they were happy to oblige. They went up the mountain and brought down a number of trees for the project. Damien himself drew up the plans and guided the natives in constructing the chapel. They were delighted to have this sturdy building in the middle of their village. They promised the priest they would keep it clean and neat. He in turn trained two of their number to read the Sunday readings and Gospels.

When he had to depart they expressed great sorrow. Just about the whole village walked and sang songs with him for the first part of his trip back home. Two of the men traveled with him all the way back to his district.

Rescue

Once as he went along the beach he saw a lifeboat from a ship drifting in the surf. As it moved closer he saw a body stretched out motionless over the tiller. He immediately swam out, ignoring the threat of sharks, and discovered eight sailors, suffering from exposure, starvation and dehydration. He got the boat to the shore and pulled the sailors into the shade, where he began to pour a small amount of coconut milk down their throats. They soon revived and told him they had escaped their burning ship to the lifeboat some eight days before. He hosted them for a few days until a ship came into port and brought the men to Honolulu.

Sorcery

Some remnants of sorcery remained on the island, and Damien began to get wind of this. When he inquired as to who was involved and where this was taking place he found his people to be tight-lipped, fearful of some bad consequences. The evil influence began to take hold of some of his parishioners, and they appeared to be less connected to the Church. The numbers of Sunday Mass-goers started to diminish.

Then, one evening as he sat outside he heard a strange sounding drum beat which suddenly stopped. The silence was broken by a sharp scream, and then quiet.

The next morning he surveyed the area and found a short, fat stone idol on a flat rock which, it seems was an altar, with stains of recently poured blood. He knocked over the idol, thereby breaking the altar. Then he tied together some branches to form a cross, and placed it where the altar had been. He left his priestly hat nearby to make sure that all would know who had torn down their false idol.

The next Sunday he denounced the idol worshipers for their foolishness. The next morning he found a weird shaped shell with horrible smelling ashes and tied with sinews in front of his door. To show his scorn for their demonic ploy, Damien took all that and attached it to the tail of a large hog. It made a rather comical image, the hog going about snorting, as it grubbed for food.

His antagonists made their move that evening by slitting the throat of the hog and leaving it at his door. He made light of it, expressing thanks to his anonymous donor for the fresh pork, but the people stayed clear out of fear.

That night he heard the drums again in the distance and a woman scratched at his window. She told him in a few fearfully cautious words that his enemies were conjuring up evil spirits to harm him. Then she ran off into the night.

He went out right away to find the source of the ominous drum beat. It took him an hour to get to the source of the noise, a burial cave on the side of a hill. There he saw about thirty men crouched down and peering into the far end of the cave. There a shriveled up old man was holding a recently killed dog, pouring its blood into a container and shrieking some strange language into it. Then, all of a sudden he held up his arm and the drumming abruptly stopped.

Then the old man reached back in the cave to bring forth a puppet of a priest, wearing a cassock and a cross around his neck. Around its waist was a rosary Damien had discovered missing some months before.

Damien had seen enough. He rushed into the crowd, which began to close in on him. He grabbed the puppet, sending the old man back into the cave. He tore the puppet to pieces with contempt, and shouted out to the participants, "Are you children that you are afraid of a doll and the blood of a dog?"

He then crushed the head of the puppet, showing that their evil spirits could do him no harm. He encouraged them to go back to their wives and children. He turned and walked back to his own house.

Growing

After this he was virtually unopposed. He built more chapels and groomed natives to preach the word when he was not present. He began schools and sought help from Honolulu for his schools. The Honolulu government was swayed by the New England missionaries to prefer Protestant schools, but they had heard of his outstanding accomplishments. So, they sent him four Catholic teachers to serve under his guidance.

He wrote to Bishop Maigret to tell him that they were outgrowing the chapels. He asked for good building materials to build a grand church. The bishop was happy to oblige, as he had heard of Damien's extraordinary work. A fund was established, and donations were requested. Just two months later the materials were ready to ship to Kohala: wood cut to size for the chapel, statues, stations of the cross, a baptismal font and other furnishings.

At one point he asked his superior in Belgium to try to get his brother Pamphile to come and join him in the mission. Instead, the leaders of the Order sent him to study for a doctorate. This was not welcomed by Damien, but it was a wise decision. After Damien died, Pamphile *did* go to Hawaii to continue his mission with the lepers. However, he could not cope with the rigors of missionary life and returned home after twenty-one months.

Damien rarely got letters from home. His parents never wrote him.

All communications went through Fr. Pamphile, who gave him news about his family and told them of Damien's activities.

When the government abandoned its antagonistic stance against Catholic schools, the young priest began to build schools. He actually got the government to help train teachers for his schools.

During his time at the Big Island, a terrible earthquake hit. The earth trembled for several days. There were avalanches from the mountains and great chasms opening in the ground to devour houses and people. Following the earthquake was a great tsunami, a tidal wave which destroyed an entire fishing village and all its residents. Then came the eruption of a volcano with its streams of glowing lava pouring down the mountain. Many of his people were injured and he helped rescue some. Then he provided food for the survivors. After that he began to rebuild.

The next year a huge hurricane hit the island, destroying two of the chapels under the jurisdiction of Fr. Gulstan, and his house as well. Damien restored all these buildings himself. He was an excellent carpenter and it is said he built about one chapel or church for each year he was serving in Hawaii.

Leprosy

A much greater threat was brewing for the Hawaiian Islands at this point: that of leprosy. In 1923 the first cases of leprosy along with smallpox were detected on the islands. By 1862 it was believed that ten to fifteen percent of the people had leprosy. A doctor at Queen's Hospital in Honolulu asked the government to take steps to quarantine the growing number of people who had contracted the disease.

In January 1865 King Kamehameha put forth a law calling for the immediate quarantine of all leprosy patients. Everyone who had the disease, including children and even infants, was to be separated from their families and communities. The people did not rush to fulfill this law which called for those with the disease to be reported to the government and put in hospitals. Government officials began to comb the villages for those afflicted, while the natives hid their relatives and friends with the disease.

In June 1865 the government decided to use the island of Molokai as the place where lepers would be sent to separate them from others. The board of health purchased land at Kalawao and Valies in September. In October it was announced that all lepers would be sent there and be cared for.

Still, the people ignored the government plan. They thought it better to care for their leprous relatives than for them to be sent away to die. Molokai became a terror-inducing word. Once it was heard by people who had lepers in their family, they would escape to the mountains, to rocky cliffs or caves, to hide.

The police went hunting the afflicted lepers and in time had to be well armed to face armed resistance from the people. At times there were gunfights and some were killed.

Nonetheless, by the end of 1866 nearly one hundred fifty of the afflicted were rounded up and put on a ship in Honolulu bound for Molokai. As the ship passed out of the harbor, the eerie sound of loud weeping could be heard far and wide. The exile of those infected was about to begin.

The board of health had in mind a place where the lepers could receive all the nurturing they needed. They hoped that those who had the strength would build homes and establish a community. This hope was aided by the fact that relatives of the afflicted were permitted at first to accompany them on the island.

However, that hope was not realized right away. There were problems with getting medicines to the island, and the provision of food was quite inadequate. What the board of health did not understand was that these people had been torn from their communities, their traditions, their families, and their beloved land. No amount of nurturing by the government could make up for that.

The government of course, had its own concerns. the population of Hawaii declined by 6,000 between 1866 and 1873, a ten percent reduction. However, during that same period, forty percent of the lepers sent to Molokai died hopelessly forgotten. The young died soon after arriving, having been treated more or less like trash in being sent there, knowing they had seen the last of their parents, and having been exploited by the other lepers who felt abandoned themselves.

One health department official brought some relief, by establishing a hospital for those near death, a home for the young and a school. But, he died before he could see these things permanently established.

In 1873, families were no longer permitted to visit their relatives on Molokai. Some food was supplied weekly, and some residents who were able, built homes. A store was established on the island.

All of this seemed to indicate that things were well on Molokai, or at least livable for the exiled lepers. But, things were not well. It was a terrible existence. The stronger residents took advantage of those near death and many gave in to drunken dancing orgies deep into the night.

A Priest for Molokai

Damien had written in a letter in April 1873 saying that he antici- pated he would eventually serve in Molokai. In May of that year Bishop Maigret met with his Hawaii priests to ask for volunteers to go to Molokai. His idea was to have several priests rotate for three month periods. Damien eagerly volunteered to go to Molokai. The bishop accepted his offer.

The other residents of the Hawaiian Islands were becoming more concerned about the conditions on Molokai. The Honolulu newspaper had recently editorialized that it would be good for King Lulalino to visit the exiles on Molokai. And, it added "If a noble Christian priest, preacher or sister should be inspired to go and sacrifice a life to console these poor wretches, that would be a royal soul to shine forever on a throne reared by human love."

On May 10, 1873 a ship left Maui with 30 lepers, some cattle for the residents, Bishop Maigret, and Father Damien. The people on Molokai joyfully greeted the ship and the bishop introduced Damien as one who "will be a father to you." Damien had chosen to "become one with you, to live and die with you." Bishop Maigret had planned for Damien to be there for just three months at a time, but his words at this time were prophetic, however unintended.

Nonetheless, the newspapers picked up the message and called Fr. Damien a hero for committing to serve on Molokai permanently. The young priest was happy at the prospect and wrote to his superior asking that the error be turned into fact, and that he be the permanent chaplain on Molokai. At the same time he asked for wine, altar bread, and all sorts of other supplies.

He asked for lumber as well so he could build himself a house. When the newspaper announced the news that the priest was in need of materials to build a house, donations came pouring in.

Protestants and non-believers saw the attention Fr. Damien was getting and wanted to get in on the action. So, they began to publish lists of ministers who had visited the people on Molokai to provide for their spiritual needs.

A number of Protestants were reluctant to help the lepers. They believed that their disease was a punishment from God for their sexual sins. Some considered leprosy as the fourth stage of syphilis.

When Damien went to Honolulu in June the Board of Health decided to issue a difficult restriction on the priest, perhaps due to the jealousy of the Protestants. The Board had not yet given permission for the priest to take up residence on Molokai. First, they allowed him to continue on the island indefinitely, but they prohibited him from serving the other (non-infected) Catholics on the island at Kalaupapa.

The hardest part of the ban, however, was that the young priest could not go to confession with another priest, something integral to a strong spiritual life and required by his Order's rule. His vice-provincial, Fr. Modeste decided to travel to Molokai to visit Damien and hear his confession. However, when Fr. Modeste attempted to go ashore, the ship's captain forbade him because of the Board of Health's strict regulations.

Damien, however, observed the conflict and rowed out to the ship hoping to board it and visit with his vice-provincial. The captain refused that as well. Damien quickly formulated another plan. He asked if anyone else beside Modeste understood French, and having been assured they did not, he called out his confession in French and received absolution.

Later Fr. Aubert decided to visit his friend Damien from his district, Kalaupapa, up the mountain on Molokai. He went down to encourage his friend and to hear his confession. When the board of health officials gave him grief after his visit, Bishop Maigret decided to move to put an end to this nonsense.

He spoke to his friends in the French consulate and they contacted the king's minister for foreign affairs. The minister spoke to the Board of Health and the results were quick: all religious ministers were to be exempt, upon making application, from the segregation laws on Molokai. Damien had no more problems from the board of health. When a new superintendent was named for the island, he did all he could to promote the welfare of the lepers and make life easier for Fr. Damien.

The Task

Damien learned from the outset that he had a huge task to accomplish among the patients. Their despair over their condition and their separation from family and friends led to their living shamelessly immoral lives. They stole from one another, refused to care for those near death, and drew the young into their opium-driven drunken orgies.

Many would curse at him as he washed their sores and provided bandages. He ignored all that. He took care of their ravaged bodies and provided them nourishment. At first the exiles received one set of clothes each year, so it was not surprising that in time they walked around in rags, the filth of which aggravated their infection and brought death more quickly.

When one of their number died he would be thrown into the ravine or buried in shallow graves where their poor bodies would become food for wild pigs. Damien put a stop to this shameful situation and made sure to be present to the dying. He made wooden coffins for the dead and began a cemetery, giving each a proper burial.

At first he slept under a Pandamus tree, but before long he made himself a small house, fifteen by twenty feet in size. It took him just eight days. He also built a storeroom to keep the many contributions he received after the newspaper article about him had appeared.

When Damien first arrived on the island, he had to walk a long way to get water. But in time they built a pipe system to bring it into the Kalawao community.

A year into his stay a hurricane destroyed all the houses owned by the wealthier patients. It turned out to be a blessing in disguise, since it gave the young priest the opportunity to start over and commence building of lovely rows of whitewashed houses. People began to take pride in their small community. By 1886 there would be over 300 houses.

He taught them to farm, cultivating sweet potatoes and other crops. In time, the number involved in farming went from just a handful to 90% of the patients.

Damien arranged for the patients to be paid for their work. Alas, the money they earned would not go far in the store, as the prices were much too high.

They began to cultivate flower gardens, and learned to play musical instruments. They began to travel by horseback, and they formed choirs to sing at Mass and other events. They were able to produce beautiful music, bringing surprised admiration from the rare visitors.

The young priest would always make his way to the harbor to greet the ships bringing their human cargo to the island. Early on there was no dock, so the patients were often pushed off the ship into the surf to try to swim ashore.

In one such incident in 1881, Damien and the others dove in the water to rescue the poor outcasts. Two of them did not make it alive and died on the beach. Damien would bring coffee and hot meals to the newcomers, and blankets as well. He arranged for them to stay in his house or the house of other residents until proper housing could be arranged.

The priest would visit each patient at least once a week. When a licensed nurse arrived at the hospital, he taught Fr. Damien all he could about drugs, bandages, hygiene, etc. In some homes he had to sweep the floors, wash the patients, launder their bed linens and bandage their wounds. He would often have to cut off rotted flesh and even amputate decayed limbs.

Quite often in the early weeks of ministering to the lepers he had to run out of a house repeatedly to throw up. He would also have severe headaches due to the horrible smell. He smoked a pipe at night to try to counteract the smells his clothing took on.

He would write to friends in Europe to ask them to send him some of the experimental drugs used there to ease the misery of the lepers. He would receive all sorts of medicines, including some Chinese remedies, to treat the patients.

Damien continued to build coffins for the dead and dig their graves himself. It was said that he made at least 600 coffins.

Many infants were torn from their mothers' arms and deposited on Molokai. Damien started an orphanage and by 1883 there were 44 little ones cared for there. He established a home for young girls and provided a woman to give them motherly attention. He started a boarding school for boys as well, which became extremely popular among the youth. He used the same kitchen as the boys' and often shared a meal with them.

The young priest was rather casual about when and what he ate. He lent out his tools freely to the patients and would eat the Hawaiian dish poi from the same bowls as they. He would also share his pipe at night as they sat around the campfire, thereby risking his own infection. Many critics later pointed how imprudent that was. And they were right it seems.

One of the characteristics of leprosy was that it affects the larynx to the point where the person could speak with barely a whisper. To hear their confession he often had to place his ear very close to the face of the penitent, thereby receiving a strong blast of their putrid breath. At other times a penitent would cough up revolting black blood on the priest. It seems he took these and other chances with infection so as to show solidarity with his people.

In 1879 Damien wrote up a schedule for himself to live each weekday on the island.

5 am rise. Go right away to the church for morning prayers including adoration and meditation.

6:30 am Mass, instruction, thanksgiving until 7:45.

8 am breakfast, a short talk and household tasks.

9 am Divine Office

9:30 spiritual reading, then study and/or letter-writing.

Noon lunch.

After lunch - visit sick and then all the Christians. (The goal is to discover the situation in each house for all in the district.)

5 pm - (if I can make it back by then) pray evening prayer (in the Divine Office) followed by house work.

6 pm - dinner

Sunset - Rosary, Divine Office, and other evening prayers.

Between 8 and 10 pm go to bed.

He would visit the nearby homes on foot, those further out by a small horse-drawn buggy given him by the board of health. There were many other activities he took up, not mentioned in his daily schedule. He helped install the water pipes so they could have a source of water nearby; he helped build a new road from his district of Kalawao to Kalaupapa; he helped improve the dock at Kalaupapa which they did by blasting away the rocks. When people's homes were blown down in hurricane winds he would rebuild them.

While he was often involved in building something for and with his patients, he was ever ready to leave that activity to go to minister to those in need. When someone was dying he would change his work clothing for his cassock, and hurry off to anoint the person.

In 1879 Fr. Damien began perpetual adoration of the Blessed Sacrament. People came to adore the Lord Jesus in the Eucharist day and night, seven days of the week. This was common practice for the priests of the Sacred Hearts, and Damien would have it on Molokai for his beloved parishioners. In that year he wrote to the superior general of his Order, "I am still happy and content among my beloved lepers of Molokai."

He also began religious associations, one for men, another for women and a third for youth. In time Damien received authorization from the Board of Health to establish orphanages near his rectory, one for boys and one for girls. By 1883 he had forty-four orphans staying there. When they grew up he arranged for the boys to learn farming, and for the girls to learn sewing and cooking. He arranged for them to marry well also.

Helpers

Over the years many different people came to volunteer to help Fr. Damien on Molokai. Fr. Andrew Burgermann arrived in 1874. He was a Sacred Hearts missionary, as was Damien, originally from the Netherlands. The visitor had come down with elephantiasis in Tahiti, and came to Hawaii to recover and to make a contribution at Molokai. He was well educated in medical techniques and Damien saw his potential to help with the patients.

However, it quickly became clear that Burgermann was extremely stubborn with the patients, and sought to have more power on the island than Damien. He courted the superintendent and his wife, and tried to arrange to become the assistant superintendent. Damien objected to the board of health, so they offered Damien the job. He took it just to avoid trouble with the new priest.

Burgermann was assigned the region of Kalaupapa, where there were no lepers. He was very interested in medicine and so was happy to come down to Damien's settlement, Kalawao and to work with the lepers. It appeared that he really wanted to be a medical doctor, and he was moving further and further away from the Order. When he confirmed that he might leave, Damien went to see him and strongly urged him to reconsider.

He did, and he remained in the Order. However, after six and a half years Burgermann left Molokai, much to the relief of Fr. Damien.

Another priest, Fr. Albert Moniton, came to serve on Molokai with Damien in 1881. Originally from France, this priest had spent twenty-four years as a missionary in the South Pacific. He had gained a good reputation there. He had given lectures throughout Europe on his work and had even been invited to meet with the Holy Father in Rome.

Upon his arrival Moniton told Damien he had been sent by their superior to investigate the rumors being spread in Hawaii that the young priest had been involved in lustful encounters with some of the patients. The visitor harangued Damien for three days solid on his alleged debaucheries. Damien remained quiet throughout all this knowing Moniton was quite mistaken.

When Damien went to perform some maintenance work on Moniton's residence in Kalaupapa, Moniton took his place at Kalawao. While there he dismissed the two women who served as cook and caretakers for the orphans in the house. He fired another woman working there as well, and made sure that no women would enter the kitchen.

Damien tried to accommodate himself to this man, but finally he wrote to his new bishop, Herman Koeckemann, to complain about his overbearing companion. He asked that Moniton be assigned somewhere else. Koeckemann ignored his letter. Then he wrote and said he would leave if he had to continue to put up with Moniton. That too was ignored.

Moniton had come to Hawaii in 1874. His elephantiasis was so revolting that the Sacred Hearts priests there could barely cope with him. Father Koeckemann, not yet named bishop, said that if Moniton remained in Honolulu, he would like to leave. In 1877 Moniton was sent to serve in Kona in the Western region of the island of Hawaii. Presumably he would have been too far from the other priests to bother them. However, apparently it was not far enough.

The vice-provincial wrote in 1879, "As for Father Albert [Moniton] nothing pleases him; everything has to be done over again, everyone is wrong, almost everyone complains about him, myself the first." He had been sent to Molokai to put him further from the missionary priests, and because the superiors felt sure his disease would not bother Damien, given what he already had to cope with.

In 1884 Moniton's condition worsened and he was permitted to go to Honolulu for treatment. He stayed at the mission with the other priests for some weeks. He had to be greased and bandaged twice each day with a most foul-smelling grease. The vice-provincial wrote that the greasing "does not stop him from being everywhere, touching everything, greasing everything. Monsignor (the bishop) has fled from him, the saintly Father Modeste has had to change places in church for air, and he pursues me repeating every day that the mission must take care of him..."

Moniton went back once again to Molokai armed with more accusations about Damien's behavior. After some time he gathered his belongings and returned to his original mission. From there he wrote to Damien to ask his forgiveness. After that, Moniton would tolerate no criticisms of Damien and came quickly to his defense when slanderous rumors were voiced in his hearing.

A Visit from The Queen

On September 15, 1881 Queen Liliuokalani came to visit Molokai. Many small boats adorned with flowers and other festive symbols went out to meet the royal steamship when it arrived in port. The choir sang beautiful Hawaiian songs. She was so moved by their welcome and by their condition that she could not read the speech she had prepared. A member of her entourage read it for her as she shed copious tears. Then Damien proceeded to take the queen on a tour of the settlement.

When Queen Liliuokalani returned to her island of Hawaii, she decreed that Damien be named a Knight Commander of the Royal Order of Kalakaua in gratitude for his outstanding work on Molokai. She asked Bishop Koeckemann to deliver the medal and official decree to Father Damien. The young priest was reticent to wear the medal, but the Bishop insisted he put it on the day he presented it.

Damien also wore it, reluctantly, on Hawaiian holidays.

Damien The Leper

In addition to shying away from honors for his work, Damien knew that this would add to the resentment his enemies had for him already. He had his own struggles to contend with at this point: he had contracted leprosy himself.

It seems he discovered his affliction during a visit to Honolulu in 1884. While at the Sacred Hearts mission center he knocked over a bowl of boiling water on his foot. He felt no pain. This sort of insensitivity in the limbs was one of the classic symptoms of leprosy. His vice-provincial, Fr. Fouesnel, saw this happen and knew what it meant. He called in a doctor immediately to make a diagnosis. The doctor confirmed that Damien now had leprosy.

Damien soon returned to Molokai and shared the news with his people. The press soon caught wind of his condition and the news quickly spread throughout the world. Shortly thereafter a family friend revealed this fact to his 83-year-old mother in Belgium. She had been shielded from the news. It broke her heart. She spent her time before a statue of the Blessed Virgin Mary and a picture of her beloved son. She never complained about his condition. Nonetheless her health declined steadily from the time she received word of his illness. She died April 6, 1886 while facing Damien's photo. When

Damien heard of her death, he was shattered.

Stoddard Visit

In 1884 Charles Warren Stoddard visited Molokai. This was his second visit, the first having occurred in 1869, several years before Damien arrived. Stoddard was a writer of considerable talent, and a friend of Robert Louis Stevenson. He had converted to Catholicism and written an account of his conversion, *A Troubled Heart and How It Was Comforted at Last.*

He was delighted to meet Damien and to see the fruits of the young priest's efforts. And he was impressed with what he called a "glow of health" and the "buoyancy of his manner." When Stoddard returned home he wrote a small book on what he found during his visit, *The Lepers of Molokai.* This proved to be a great help in stirring those who read it to send all sorts of aid to Fr. Damien.

Stoddard was very happy to have visited Damien. After leaving he wrote to the priest to say he was a bit jealous of the life he led. He wrote, "You seemed to be happy, much happier than those who live in the world."

Visit to Honolulu

For some time Damien had been requesting permission to visit

Honolulu for treatment in the hospital there and go to confession as well, something which weighed heavily on his heart. He asked twice in fact, once in 1884 and once again in 1885. Both times Fr. Foesnel refused him.

This has to be seen in the context of what sort of publicity was being given to Damien's mission. It seems he had written his brother Pamphile from time to time, telling him what was happening in Molokai. His brother had turned over some of the letters to the press in Europe, and as a result Damien's work with the lepers became widely known. Damien was not happy to have his letters used in this way and urged his brother to stop doing this.

The fact that Damien needed more supplies than were forthcoming from the Board of Health created political problems for the board and for the bishop and Fr. Foesnel, Damien's vice-provincial. This, and the fact that Damien could be quite insistent on his needs in the settlement when dealing with the Hawaiian government, soured his relationship with his bishop and vice-provincial. This hurt him very much, as he had had a good relationship with their predecessors.

In any case, Damien was refused permission because the bishop, the vice-provincial, and the Prime Minister believed it would look bad for this famous (by now) priest who had leprosy to show up in the capital. He was told that it would embarrass the whole mission. When the afflicted priest continued to ask, Fr. Foesnel wrote back to him saying that if he came to Honolulu it would show he was "an egoist, without delicacy or charity." This, as Damien wrote, gave him "more pain than everything I have had to suffer since my childhood."

The doctor in Kalawao (Molokai) had encouraged Damien's visit to Honolulu for treatment and for a little rest and relaxation. He wrote to Bishop Koeckemann on Damien's behalf urging him to give permission. It seems that a number of messages crisscrossed between Kalawao and Honolulu in early July 1886.

Believing he saw a certain softening in the prohibition against his going, Damien finally went to Honolulu on July 10. He was not certain he was in the right for going, but he was never reprimanded by either Fouesnel or Koeckemann.

Once there the afflicted priest pursued some business for his mission and part of that was to meet with Sister Marianne Cope. He was hoping she would send some of her sisters of St. Francis to Molokai.

She had come with six of her sisters in 1883 to serve in the hospital for lepers in Kakaako, Honolulu. All were impressed with the efficiency and expertise with which the sisters performed their duties. Most were trained nurses. They cleaned and cleaned the hospital which was abysmally filthy.

Sister Leopoldina Burns wrote of what they found:

Fat bedbugs nested in the cracks (of walls). Brown stains upon walls, floors, and bedding showed where their blood-filled bodies had been crushed by desperate patients. Straw mattresses, each more or less covered by a dirty blanket, lay upon the unswept floor. ... Blankets, mattresses, clothing, and patients all supported an ineradicable population of lice"

The sisters also established a school and a hospital on Maui.

Why didn't the sisters go to Molokai right away upon reaching Hawaii? It seems that the hospital in Kakaako was very close to Honolulu and Waikiki, and was really an eyesore for the Hawaiian leaders. They wanted the sisters there because this hospital, in plain sight of all the visitors to Honolulu, was bad politics. And, to make things worse, the Prime Minister, Walter Murray Gibson was infatuated with Mother Marianne.

Some of the Sisters had been concerned before coming about catching leprosy themselves. Mother Marianne set their minds at ease saying, "...you will never be a leper, nor will any Sister of our Order." In fact, to this day none of the Franciscan sisters serving the lepers in Hawaii has ever contracted the disease.

Sister Marianne did such great work in Honolulu that the lepers in her hospital were not exiled to Molokai. However, when a new government took over in 1887 they would begin to enforce more strictly the quarantine laws. They would close the hospital, and send the lepers to Molokai. Mother Marianne would choose to follow them there.

While in Honolulu Damien met Doctor Masanao Goto, who had come up with a novel treatment for leprosy. This included frequent baths and special pills. Damien made use of these aids and found them helpful. He said his hand was better and he regained some of his strength. He arranged for these treatments to be administered on Molokai.

Brother Joseph

Damien stayed just briefly in Honolulu and was back in Molokai July 19 when a ship arrived bringing more lepers. He always tried to meet these ships to give them a warm welcome to soften the blow of their arrival in this sad place. Also on the ship that day was a 43-year-old American by the name of Ira Barnes Dutton. In time he came to be known as "Brother Joseph."

Brother Joseph joined the army in 1861 to fight in the Civil War. His army career was quite successful and he was honorably discharged as a captain in 1866. He married a woman he met during the war, and she turned his life into a nightmare: soon after they married she went to live with another man, but she continued to spend his money, sending him into serious debt. He divorced her and promptly became an alcoholic. After a few years he "took the pledge" against drinking and never drank alcohol again.

In 1883 Dutton converted to Catholicism and changed his name to

Joseph (his favorite saint). He went to live with the Trappist monks at Gethsemane in Kentucky. He loved it there and in the silence of the monastery, he found his bearings, and did penance for his past sins. He stayed about a year and a half, at which time he decided his vocation was to involve active charity, rather than the contemplative life.

After he left Gethsemane he happened to read about Fr. Damien and his ministry on Molokai. He knew very quickly that this was his calling. He left San Francisco in 1886 and arrived in Honolulu in early July. Having received permission from Bishop Koeckemann and the head of the Board of Health, he arrived at Molokai July 19 as we mentioned earlier. He wanted no salary, but was nonetheless given one by the Hawaiian government. He had come to serve there, to do penance, as he said, for his many past sins.

Damien was most happy to have Brother Joseph. He built him a small house, close to his own house. Dutton proved to be a most capable and energetic worker. In turn, he was amazed at the limitless energy he saw in Damien. It is said that they sometimes worked from 4:30 am to 11 pm.

Fr. Damien admired his new assistant so much that he suggested he get ordained a priest. Dutton shied away from the very possibility. When Damien was persistent in his suggestion, Dutton told him he was unworthy of the priesthood. Damien persisted. Dutton refused. Finally, Brother Joseph told Damien why he felt unworthy, something which remained a secret between the two. The secret was never revealed, but Damien made no more mention of the priesthood.

Brother Joseph was a polite, gentle servant of the lepers. He seemed to have endless patience with all. He was present when Damien died and he gave witness to the wholesomeness of the priest's life against those few who slandered him after his death.

Dutton developed a certain degree of fame himself after Damien died. He corresponded with kings, presidents and even Thomas Edison. He asked President Teddy Roosevelt to send the American naval fleet by Molokai as a way of honoring the patients on Molokai. The president was happy to comply with Joseph's request and the ships appeared in the harbor in 1908, bringing great joy to all on the island.

Damien's Decline

It was said that in the years just prior to his coming down with leprosy, Damien seemed a bit soured by all the trials he had getting more cooperation in doing his work on Molokai. However, once he caught the disease, he appeared to be more joyful and upbeat. It seems he did not want his people to think he was sad to have become one of them.

By early 1888 Damien's condition had worsened considerably. On his front and back, his arms and legs leprous lumps had formed; his nose, mouth and larynx were affected; swelling had appeared on his nose, lips, forehead and chin; he became quite thin and weak.

He continued to receive unkind messages from his superiors as they continued to receive charitable donations from all quarters. This continued to stoke the fires of their irritation at this priest who (unintentionally) was making them look bad. The priest tried to cope with this stream of disapproving words by writing spiritual reminders for himself such as the following:

Pray to achieve the spirit of humility so as to desire scorn. If one is scorned may one rejoice in it. Let us not be touched by the praises of men; let us not be self-satisfied; let us be grateful to those who cause us pain or treat us with scorn, and pray to God for them. To accomplish this, beyond grace, there is needed a great self-abnegation and a continual mortification: by these one finds oneself transformed into Christ crucified. St. John of the Cross always prayed, "Lord, may I be scorned for love of You." Let us make frequent meditations on the scorn Christ suffered before Pilate–the face covered with spittle–the crown of thorns–the reed–the scarlet cloak–Barrabas is preferred, etc.

Help from England

In February 1888 an Anglican priest from London, Rev. Hugh Chapman read about Damien's mission on Molokai and decided he wanted to help. He wrote to Damien and offered to raise money for the lepers. Damien was delighted at the prospect and wrote back to graciously accept the help and to mention that Brother Joseph, his assistant, was a former Anglican.

Once he heard from Damien, Chapman mentioned the idea to his parishioners in London and they set about to raise funds for the lepers. He began to send articles about the effort to the newspapers in London. He also was able to interest the Catholic archbishop of Westminster, Henry Manning, who was most willing to lend support.

All of this brought criticism to Chapman and Damien as well. Some letters to the editor suggested the lepers were better off left to die than to be fed the Catholic faith and lose their souls as a result. Still others claimed that the lepers were just being punished for the sinful life they led in Hawaii.

Despite all this furor, Chapman was able to raise a good deal of money for the mission on Molokai. He raised nine hundred pounds ($4,800) in the first three months. In three years the total grew to 2600 pounds.

The newspapers in Hawaii heard of the charitable gifts and questioned the need for such aid. Didn't the government do enough for the patients? And if it did, what would the money be used for? Americans, who looked to annex Hawaii to the United States were uncomfortable with the British sending help to Molokai.

Another Englishman who helped Damien's mission was Edward Clifford, a wealthy philanthropist. He had nothing but hostility for the Catholic religion. But when he read an article about Damien in a magazine, and heard of Chapman's efforts, he wanted to meet this hero of the lepers. And, of course, he wanted to help.

So he paid a visit to Molokai in December, 1888. He brought all sorts of gifts with him. Among the gifts was a magnificent watercolor picture of St. Francis. It held great meaning for Damien since St. Francis and his friars used to regularly visit the lepers and care for them.

It also had symbolic value to the patients, since Damien, in imitation of St. Francis, would go out daily with various sorts of food and feed the birds. He gave a familiar whistle and all sorts of birds appeared, landing on his hat, his shoulders, or his arms and allowed him to feed them.

Preparing for Death

Once he was diagnosed with leprosy, Damien prayed that the disease would not overcome him quickly while he had so much yet to do. He also worried about how his patients would be treated once he died. He feared they might not send a father figure to provide for them, but rather some distant authority figure.

His ear formed a leprous sore, and his eyebrows disappeared. He began to experience severe fatigue. He pushed himself by day, being oblivious to how tired he was becoming by the interest in his work. But, by night he shed copious tears over his exhaustion. He was experiencing burnout it seems.

A New Helper

He wrote to Bishop Koeckemann and Fr. Foesnel about his state of mind. Alas, he received back no messages of consolation. He realized he would have to go this without their support. He found comfort in praying the rosary in the graveyard, among those he had prayed for at their deaths.

Damien begged his vice-provincial Fr. Fouesnel and Bishop Koeckemann to send him another priest as an assistant, especially when he caught leprosy. In the Rule of the order we find, "The general rule is that no member of the community, whether a priest or brother, will be sent out or remain on the islands alone."

Father Conrady

Finally Father Lambert Conrady, a Belgian parish priest wrote to

Damien volunteering to come and assist him. Damien was delighted at the prospect so he wrote to Bishop Koeckemann and Fr. Foesnel asking permission to invite him. Neither liked the idea, but finally the bishop agreed grudgingly. The new priest arrived on Molokai in May 1888.

It seems that the bishop felt that having another Belgian on Molokai made it appear that only Belgians would opt for this difficult assignment. So he sent out a plea to all the missionaries in Hawaii, seeking a volunteer to go to Molokai. Almost every priest volunteered. It would be several more months before a priest was sent.

Fr. Conrady stayed in Molokai until six years after the death of Damien. Early on the new priest endured headaches–as had Damien, due to the horrible stench of the patients. Undeterred, he got used to this after a time, the headaches ended and he was able to befriend the lepers.

When he left Molokai, he intended to establish a leper colony in Canton, China. But, to do so he needed to be a medical doctor, according to officials. So, he studied for and attained a medical degree at the University of Oregon in just five years. He graduated at age 60.

He was not yet ready for his mission: he had to raise money to do it. From 1900 to 1908 he went about preaching in various countries including Belgium, the United States and Canada. During that time he amassed thirty thousand dollars for his mission, while inspiring over 200 missionary vocations by his fiery sermons.

Then, he pushed on to Canton. There he established a leprosy hospital and served for six years among the lepers. He was well loved there for his warmhearted dedication to the patients. When he died of pneumonia in 1914, his leprosy hospital had seven hundred lepers.

The End

Bishop Koeckemann warmed up to Damien as the afflicted priest's end approached in early 1889. He wrote him some kind letters, but he made no attempt to be with Damien on his deathbed. He wanted to avoid any political issues. Fr. Fouesnel offered no such kindness, sending strongly negative letters a month before Damien died.

As time went on he suffered more symptoms: he had leprous sores all over; infected swelling afflicted his nose, eyes, and larynx. The latter swelling prevented him from being able to sleep more than two hours a night. Despite that, he continued to get up and work vigorously the next day.

He lost his eyesight as well, and so had to have others read to him in the evening. He continued to pray the Divine Office (the collection of Psalms and other prayers required of religious), but in time, even this had to be read to him. This he listened to intently, in addition to the lives of the saints and other spiritual books.

He developed a bad fever and began to fail miserably. Nevertheless, in November (1888), when it was announced that Mother Marianne and her Franciscan sisters were arriving at the port to come and serve at Molokai, he immediately got up and welcomed them and showed them around the settlement. This fulfillment of his long-time prayer seemed to energize him. Before long he was visiting his people and even seen atop a building installing a new roof.

Once the sisters arrived, Fr. Wendelin Moellers, another Sacred Hearts priest, was sent by the bishop to the island to be their chaplain and confessor. Fr. Damien finally had a priest from his own order, which he had requested for so many years.

Damien had a letter written to Fr. Foesnel asking the Sacred Hearts sisters to make him a funeral pall. Alas, he received a nasty response. Nonetheless, a funeral pall did arrive.

He began to have constant diarrhrea and incessant coughing. His nose had fallen apart so his glasses rested precipitously on his frazzled ears.

On March 19, 1889 he took to his bed. He was found on the floor shivering with fever as he never used a bed. This time they convinced him to rest in a real bed. On March 28 he had to remain in bed permanently. He made his last confession on March 30.

Fr. Wendelin wrote of Damien at this time:

Saturday, the thirtieth, he prepared for death. It was truly edifying to see him. He seemed so happy. After I had heard his general confession I made my confession to him. Then we renewed our vows which bind us to the congregation. The following day he received the holy viaticum (final holy Communion). During the day he was bright and cheerful as usual. "Look at my hands," he said. "All the wounds are closing and the crust is turning black. That is the sign of imminent death. I am not mistaken for I have seen many lepers die."

He was hoping his end would come soon, but it didn't. He was too strong for a quick exit. On April 13 he took on another fever, and two days later, in the early morning hours, April 15, 1889 he died in the arms of Fr. Conrady and brother Sinnett (an American nurse who arrived in 1888). Sinnett wrote, "I have never seen a happier death. He constantly was one with God through his prayer and suffering."

He had served for sixteen years on Molokai. He had a smile on his face and by the time he was dressed for burial the leprous marks on his face had disappeared.

His death reverberated around the world. His courageous commitment to the least of Christ's brothers and sisters helped the world realize that leprosy was a sickness borne by human beings, who were not to be stripped of their human dignity. When he himself died of the disease it put the lie to those who mistakenly saw leprosy as a punishment for the sins of those afflicted.

Messages of condolences poured in from all corners of the world from presidents, national leaders, and many, many others. Damien was dressed in his Mass vestments for burial. The funeral took place at St. Philomena's church and he was buried under the Pandamus tree where he stayed when he first arrived on Molokai.

After Damien's Death

Once Damien died, things on Molokai regressed. In July the nurse James Sinnett wrote to Edward Clifford,

Following the death of our dear leper-priest there has been a complete change in the order of things here. It is no longer an institution where children learn virtue. They no longer have the salutary fear of Father Damien. Drunkards have recommenced drinking; distillers to distill, and disorders have reappeared among the young people.

One year later some of the lepers began to stir up trouble. They bound up the administrator of the settlement with ropes, and threatened to bind up Fr. Conrady as well. After things died down, Fr. Wendelin sensed a continuing unrest among an unruly group on the island. In 1890 Fr. Wendelin wrote to a friend, "How I admire Father

Damien... He has lived among a people that were more than ungrateful, and more than libertine."

Nevertheless, some very good things began to happen after Damien's death: within twenty years any number of hospitals for lepers were started throughout the world. In virtually every region where lepers lived, missionaries were moved to begin such a ministry.

Many of those who served in this capacity claimed Father Damien as the motivating factor in their vocation. Damien's Congregation of the Sacred Hearts saw an increase in vocations to their Order as well. In 1870 they had 451 members; in 1890 just 350. During the ten years after Damien died, there were 251 new members. Fr. Wendelin was sure this was due to the influence of Damien.

Damien's body rested in Molokai until 1936. It seems that in the early 1930s the village of Kalawao was to be abandoned and the residents moved to Kalaupapa. The Church in Belgium did not want the grave of Damien to remain in an uninhabited place and be ignored. So, King Leopold sought permission from President Roosevelt to have the body returned from Hawaii (by then a US territory) to Belgium. The request was granted.

On January 27, 1936 the body was taken from its grave and put on a ship to Honolulu. After a brief stop there, with special honors, it was sent on to San Francisco for more honors, and then sent on to Belgium. It arrived there May 3, and after much fanfare was buried in Louvain. It is now in a chapel of the Sacred Hearts Order, where it receives a large number of visitors every year.

India

In 1964, a new complex was started in Dahnbad, India to care for the many lepers in India. Inspired by the work of Damien, it was named the Damien Social Welfare Center. It included three hospitals, a leprosy control system and a rehabilitation center for those afflicted by the disease.

The workers at these facilities were called "Damiens" and were particularly devoted to caring for the young patients. By 1981 they were serving nearly 24,000 persons.

Slander

In August 1889, just a few months after Damien died, a Congregational minister in Honolulu, Rev. Charles McEwen Hyde wrote to a friend in Australia, Rev. H. B. Gage, about the now-famous priest. It was in answer to the friend's inquiry about the holy man of Molokai.

In the letter Hyde wrote regarding Damien:

The simple truth is, he was a coarse, dirty man, headstrong and bigoted. He was not sent to Molokai, but went there without orders; did not stay at the leper settlement (before he became one himself), but circulated freely over the whole island (less than half the island is devoted to the lepers), and he came often to Honolulu. He had no hand in the reforms and improvements inaugurated, which were the work of our Board of Health, as occasion required and means were provided. He was not a pure man in his relations with women, and the leprosy of which he died should be attributed to his vices and carelessness. Others have done much for the lepers, our own ministers, the government physicians, and so forth, but never with the Catholic idea of meriting eternal life...

Unfortunately when Gage received this letter, he passed it on to the *Sydney Presbyterian*, where Robert Louis Stevenson happened to see it. It seems that Hyde had written words of glowing praise for Damien in the *Honolulu Gazette* only four years prior to writing this letter. It is quite unclear how his opinion could have changed so dramatically in four years.

Stevenson, upon reading this highly critical letter about Damien decided to do some of his own investigating. He had never met Damien while he was still alive, but traveled to Molokai shortly after he read Hyde's letter. He stayed just over a week, during which time he interviewed people on the island. He avoided those who loved Damien and who admired him, but sought out those who had been at odds with him, or those Protestants who had been antagonistic toward him. They reported that he could be "strong headed and officious" and often wore a dirty cassock, because he quite often spent the day building homes for the patients. At the start of the day his cassock was clean.

A year later Stevenson was visiting Australia and a person brought up Hyde's letter about Damien. The poet took up his pen and wrote a scathing letter debunking virtually every negative point made in Hyde's letter. He made sure his letter was printed in just about every newspaper in the United States and Europe. He won the day rather handily.

However, four years later, when Stevenson died, the supporters of the slander brought forth the lies again and claimed that Stevenson had retracted his words just before he died. When that lie began to be spread, Stevenson's wife made it clear in an interview that no such retraction had ever been made. The poet was unrelenting in his convictions about the slanderers.

Honors

In 1969 Damien was honored for having performed great humanitarian service and had a statue of him erected in the Rotunda of the Capitol in Washington, DC. Among the speeches given was that of Bishop John Scanlan of Honolulu. He spoke glowingly of Fr.

Damien but one part of his speech was telling in terms of the human reality of this dedicated missionary:

> Damien, human in his short temper and impatience, but with the mark of divinity in his loving concern for the most wretched of men and women, speaks now from this seat of civil government of the Nation, and the word that he utters is the Hawaiian word which expresses what is noblest and greatest in us all–aloha.

Canonization

Shortly after Damien's death the superior general of the Order of the Sacred Hearts decided to bring up the possibility of Damien being canonized. He commissioned Bishop Koeckemann to arrange for all who knew Damien to be interviewed. Koeckemann appointed the priests Fr. Wendelin Moellers and Fr. Corneille Limburg (who had served at Kalaupapa) to gather the information.

Fr. Corneille provided this summary:

> Father Damien sacrificed his life for the poor lepers. Everyone knows that; everyone rightly admires that. If however, one looks into the details of his everyday life, the details of his various virtues, then you find nothing extraordinary. Just as

with others you find many shortcomings. As regards special favors or miracles obtained due to his intercession, there are none.

Bishop Koeckemann sent on the report to the Order's headquarters in April 1890, adding his own opinion: "You will see that the result has nothing brilliant. But we can trust entirely in the reporter's judgement and truthfulness."

This report brought the process to a standstill. Damien, it seemed just wasn't a saint, or so it seemed at this point.

However, as time went on, the story of Father Damien spread and the regard for him grew. Brother Dutton had predicted this, saying, "All of the complaints that one can make about Father Damien will soon disappear; what will remain will be the figure of a saint–his qualities will only grow."

The second investigation into the life of Fr. Damien to determine his worthiness to be canonized began in Malines, Belgium in 1938. This preliminary procedure resulted in a report sent to the Congregation of Rites in Rome in 1941.

In 1955 Pope Pius XII officially introduced Damien's cause. Many witnesses were called in 1956 and 1957 to give their opinion of his virtues, and they were quite positive. It seemed clear to some of the witnesses that without a good deal of supernatural help Damien could never have done what he did for these poor, condemned people. It was noted that even many years after his death there was much devotion and attachment among the lepers for this man. Many, many lepers came to reflect at his empty grave on Molokai.

The study continued for many years and included many criticisms of Damien's roughness and his problems with his superiors. Much was written in response to these criticisms as well. When a vote was taken in February 1969 five voted for continuing the process, seven against. Thus, things stopped again.

Two months later Pope Paul VI reopened the case. Much more research was done and new information surfaced. The new data included facts about the shortcomings of Bishop Koeckemann and Fr. Fouesnel. When another vote was taken in 1976 all nine of those reviewing the data voted for moving on toward canonization.

In 1977 Pope Paul VI proclaimed that Damien's life was of "heroic virtue" and he was thus declared Venerable. This is the first step towards canonization.

At this time a collection of thirty-three thousand signatures of lepers from many different countries who requested consideration for Damien's canonization was given to Pope Paul. Of the thirty-three thousand who signed the petition just nine thousand were Catholic. Three hundred two Catholic bishops added their support.

One of his staunch supporters was Mother Teresa of Calcutta. In 1984 she wrote to Pope John Paul II, urging him to raise up a saint to inspire her sisters to continue to strive in their mission to the poor, naming Damien as an ideal person to fill that role.

Damien needed one miracle to be beatified. It would be the healing of sister Simplicia Hue which had occurred many years previously. In 1895 this Sacred Hearts sister was enduring a painful intestinal malady, which, she was told, would eventually bring about her death. She and her fellow sisters began a novena to Fr. Damien and she was healed overnight. This was the miracle needed to beatify Damien.

On June 4, 1995 Pope John Paul II beatified Damien in Brussels, Belgium at the Basilica of the Sacred Heart. Shortly thereafter the hand of the new Blessed was returned to Kalaupapa as a relic to be buried there.

For canonization a new miracle was necessary occurring after the beatification. In early 1998 eighty-year-old Audrey Toguchi was diagnosed with an aggressive type of cancer, liposarcoma. From April until June she received radiation treatments to try to arrest the growth of this rare disease. An examination in September revealed that the cancer had spread to both lungs. The doctors told her she could get chemotherapy to slow the growth, but even with that she had no more than six months to live.

Audrey rejected chemotherapy and said she would pray to Fr. Damien. On October 2, 1998 she returned for another exam. The doctor was surprised to see that the tumor had shrunk. It continued to show shrinkage in the months that followed. He asked her what treatment she was taking and she replied she was just praying to Fr.

Damien. In May 1999 the tumor had entirely disappeared. The doctor, although he was not Catholic, suggested she write to the Holy Father about her cure.

When the doctors were questioned about the likelihood of this cancer disappearing after having spread, they indicated that 80% of patients died within six to twelve months. Experts at Memorial Sloan-Kettering Cancer Center in New York were completely in accord with those who found this cure inexplicable. They noted that of 135 patients having the same diagnosis as Toguchi 100% died within three years.

Still, the Church moved slowly. In 2005 and 2007 further tests were made. Finally, on July 3, 2008 Pope Benedict made it known that nothing stood in the way of Damien's canonization.

On October 11, 2009 Pope Benedict XVI canonized Fr. Damien in Rome. Forty thousand people attended in St. Peter's Square, including more than 500 Hawaiians. Among the crowd were many lepers, and cancer-free Audrey Toguchi.

His feast day was set as May 10, the day in 1873 when Damien first set foot on Molokai to serve the lepers.

Postscript

Brother Dutton continued on long after Damien died. He never left Molokai again, and loved working with the lepers. He said he was deeply impressed by their courage, and could not imagine working anywhere else. He died on March 26, 1931 at the age of 87.

Mother Marianne Cope continued her work on Molokai with several of her sisters. After Damien died, she was able to raise donations to provide more education for the people.

She continued Damien's house for the men and boys, and initiated a house to care for women and young girls. She continued until her death on August 9, 1918 at the age of 80. She was beatified on May 15, 2005 and canonized on October 21, 2012.

After Damien's death both Bishop Koeckemann and Fr. Foesnel defended him against the slanderous attack by Rev. Charles Hyde. In February 1892 the Bishop endured a stroke which left him paralyzed and unconscious. He died shortly thereafter on February 22, 1892. Father Fouesnel died later that year.

Hawaii continued as a kingdom until 1893 when American residents peacefully overthrew the monarchy. The queen gave up her throne, but under protest. President Grover Cleveland initially sided with the monarchy and recommended that the queen be restored to power. However, an investigation of the Senate Foreign Relations Committee produced a report claiming that the US soldiers had not acted unjustly and that the queen should not be restored to power. Not all were convinced that the report was fair.

Amid continuing controversy, Hawaii was annexed in 1898 as a territory of the US. It became the fiftieth state in 1959.

Reflection

Damien de Veuster was a priest with many talents. He was able to work long hours, he was strong, and he loved being a priest. When offered the opportunity to work with the world's most abandoned outcasts, the lepers of Molokai, he eagerly volunteered. He saw himself as a father to these poor people and so treated them like his own children. No doubt he felt he could not remain aloof from them, even if that put him at risk for catching their disease. The lepers knew he would give his all for them, and as a result they responded to his call for them to change and live upright and moral lives.

He had strained relationships with his superiors near the end of his life and could be hard-headed with the people who served along side him. He was also considered too insistent on getting the help he needed from the Board of Health.

Nonetheless, the overarching principle of his life was to serve and lift up those who had a debilitating, disgusting disease, and help them to realize their own human dignity and call to holiness, despite their illness. For this great and noble effort, he was declared a saint, despite his shortcomings.

His story brings to mind that of St. Jerome (who could be quite sarcastic at times) and St. Padre Pio (who could be gruff at times). Despite his personality flaws, one would have to admit that Damien was remarkably heroic in taking on the mission he chose, heroically loving. And as St. Peter wrote, "Love covers a multitude of sins" (1 Pet 4:8). Thanks be to God for this holy man, saint of God.

Sources

Bunson, Margaret and Matthew, *Apostle of The Exiled: St. Damien of Molokai*, Huntington, IN: Our Sunday Visitor, 2009, pp. 41-50, 197.

Christensen, Jen, "Mother Marianne becomes an American saint," CNNhttp://www.cnn.com/2012/10/20/health/saint-mariannecope.

Daws, Gavan, *Holy Man; Father Damien of Molokai*, Honolulu: University of Hawaii Press, 1973, pp. 60-109.

DeVolder, Jan, *The Spirit of Father Damien*, English tr. by John Steffen, San Francisco: Ignatius Press, 2010, pp. 61-171.

Farrow, John, *Damien The Leper*, New York: Sheed and Ward, 1937, pp. 142-205.

"Mother Marianne Cope's Legacy in Hawaii" http://www.stfrancishawaii.org/mission/our-patron-saint/the-story-of-st-marianne.

Chapter Two

St. Margaret of Cortona

(1247-1297)

St. Margaret was born in Laviano, Italy in 1247. Her mother raised her and her brother Bartholomew with great love and tenderness, and taught them to love God and seek a life of virtue. Thus, her mother's death when Margaret was only seven was a tragic blow.

Her father, a farmer, remarried two years later. He was weak and soft on her at times—spoiling Margaret in the process—and excessively violent at others. His new wife had no use for his lively, strong-willed daughter, and attempted with harshness to undo the spoiling her husband had accomplished.

Seeking Love

Caught between her parents' extremes, neither of whom provided the love and affection she had known and which she so desperately wanted, she sought love outside her home. As so often happens with a girl who does not experience adequate love from her father, she looked to the boys of her town for love.

They were quick to respond as she was strikingly beautiful. Her looks, combined with her spirited nature made her irresistible to them. She loved the attention, and to keep it gave in to their sinful desires. Before she was 17 the whole town knew of her sexual adventures.

Mistress

At 17 she was noticed by a nobleman passing through the town and he arranged to meet her. For him it was love at first sight. He offered her gifts and invited her to come live with him in his castle in the hills of Montepulciano. Margaret turned him down, pointing out she was from a poor family and of a much lower class. He suggested that her beauty was worth more than riches, and would be enough for him to marry her. This lie convinced her and off she went. Perhaps she had decided it was time to move on, to get away from the contempt of the women, the sexual advances of the men.

He never fulfilled his promise of marriage, so for the next nine years she lived with him unmarried. Her sinful life shocked the entire region. She added insult to injury by often riding through the town on a magnificent horse dressed in expensive jewels and fancy clothes. When she gave birth to a son, Margaret gave up on the hope of marriage and resigned herself to her situation.

Not surprisingly, in spite of her somewhat glamorous life, Margaret was often unhappy. She would find an out-of-the-way room in the castle and say to herself, "How good it would be to pray here! ...How well one would do penance here!" She would sit there and cry over her sins, hoping some day to repent and receive God's forgiveness and mercy. Years later, after her conversion, she said, "At Montepulciano I lost honor, dignity and peace; I lost everything but faith." No doubt she kept her faith, if not hope and love, because of the holy efforts of her mother, who often came to her mind.

One day a friend pleaded with her, "You wretch, how much lower will you bring yourself?" She placed her hands over her eyes and let out a miserable cry. Then, almost as if she saw herself in a crystal ball, she proclaimed, "Don't worry! The day will come when you will call me a saint, because I will have become so holy!"

She would give generously to the poor to soothe her troubled conscience. When she was greeted politely in the streets, she sometimes was moved to respond that such an honor was better than she was due in light of her evil ways.

For nine years Margaret continued her sinful life, torn between pleasure and guilt, comfort and disgust. She felt trapped. She hid her agony from her lover and others in the house. It was only through tragedy that she was released from her terrible situation.

When she was 26 her nobleman one day didn't come home from a business trip on time. After two days of waiting she was led by his dog to his bloodstained, murdered body, covered by some branches and leaves in the woods. She cried out in horror and fainted on the spot.

When she came to, she faced squarely the issue of her own death, of divine judgement. Where was her lover's soul now? Was it her fault? Where would she end up for all eternity?

Breaking Free

She resolved to change her life and go home to her father. Dressed in the clothes of a penitent sinner, she took her young son and walked to Laviano. There, she threw herself at the feet of her father and asked forgiveness and shelter. He gave her both, at first.

However, when her stepmother heard of it, she wouldn't *think* of it! Her father gave in to his wife, and sent his daughter away.

She walked away leading her young, weeping son, uncertain where she would go. She stopped under a tree and tried to think. She considered returning to the comfort of her past sinful life. The devil tempted her: "Come back to me. Return to the pleasures of life. You still have your beauty, your youth, your wit... You shall have love, and the world will again pour into your cup delightful pleasures. You will not have to be down on yourself, as your parents have driven you out." It was an alluring thought.

All of a sudden she caught herself, saying, "No, no, Margaret. Don't give your life to shame and regret. You have long enough dishonored your Creator. Long enough have you fought against Him who redeemed you with His blood... Your earthly father has rejected you but your heavenly Father will receive you." She felt moved to go to Cortona and seek refuge with the Franciscans, who were known for their kindness toward repentant sinners. Off they went on foot toward Cortona, 12 miles away.

At the city gate they came upon two kind noblewomen who saw her miserable, tired face, and made friends with her. She told them of her sinful life and of her desire to reform. They were moved by her story and took her and her son to live with them.

Mercy

Soon they brought her to the Franciscan house. There she confessed her sins, pouring out her heart. The holy Franciscan priest, Fr. Giunta, told her of God's tremendous mercy, and how good it was that she had turned away from her former ways. As he gave her absolution she found the peace she had sought for so long.

She humbly asked entry into the Third Order of the Franciscans, that she might do penance for the rest of her life. She was accepted on a trial basis to see if her conversion would be permanent. Fr. Giunta was to be her spiritual director during her trial period, which would last three years.

She attended Mass each day, spent long hours in prayer, worked as a midwife nurse, helping deliver babies, and cared for the poor. She resolved to conquer her body, which, she said, had conquered her. She went to Fr. Giunta with a sharp blade, prepared to scar her beautiful face, which had helped bring her down. The priest would not hear of it. She wanted to be called "the poor sinner," or "the great sinner" by all.

She felt the urge to do public penance for her sins, and proposed to her director that she go to Montepulciano, where she had lived in sin for so long, to seek forgiveness of the people. She wanted to go there wearing rags, with her hair shaved off, and her face covered. She would have a woman lead her around the town by a rope, saying, "Look at this terrible sinner, who by her vanity, pride and scandals has ruined so many souls in this city."

Again, Fr. Giunta refused her request. He did, however, allow her to go back to her home town, Laviano, for a lesser display of penitence. After Mass, before the whole congregation gathered there, she appeared with a rope at her neck and threw herself down before a woman of the nobility whose godly advice she had always scorned, and begged forgiveness for her shameful behavior. She was so humble and sorrowful in her request that many began to weep.

The woman was so moved by this display of contrition that she brought Margaret to her house and heard the young woman tell her how wonderful the Third Order of Franciscans was. Margaret was so convincing that the noblewoman agreed to join herself.

Franciscan at Last

After Margaret had spent three years in great prayer and penance, Father Giunta agreed she was ready to join the Franciscans. In 1276, at the age of 29, Margaret entered the Third Order of Penance of St. Francis.

She made three resolutions: to beg for all the money she needed to live on (and give any excess away); to do twice as many penances; and to ask of the woman who was providing her shelter, for a more miserable and private room in which to live. After she sent her son off to school, she was given a small shack next to the Franciscan church. She began to live a life of deep penance, wearing rags for clothing, sleeping on the ground with a stone or piece of wood as a pillow, and seeking to humiliate herself in every possible way.

She ate only a slice of bread and some water with some uncooked vegetables. She denied herself all comforts, wearing a hairshirt and whipping herself to bring under control the body which for so long had held her prisoner to sin. She spent most nights meditating on the sufferings of Christ and shedding tears for her past sins.

Every day she would go early to the church to pray the Divine Office with the Franciscans and attend their Mass. She took Holy Communion every day. Then she would meditate on the "book of love," namely the crucifix, the book "written in every language... or, better, the language of the heart... with the blood of Christ." In the evenings she would return to the church for prayer, sometimes continuing through the night.

When she was at prayer in the church the Lord began to speak plainly to her. As she prayed one night in the empty church, she poured our her heart in prayer with words such as , "My God, you have suffered so much for me, will you forgive me?" She immediately heard a voice from the crucifix say, "What do you want, my poor sinner?"

She replied, "Lord Jesus, I seek only You."

She thought about the title Jesus gave her, "my poor sinner." She wondered if she still had more to make up for her sins after her years of prayer and penance. She turned to St. Francis of Assisi, asking him to pray for her before God that by her prayer and fasting the debt of her sins would be completely removed. Less than a week later, after receiving holy communion, Margaret heard a voice within her describing her life and then saying, "I, the Son of the Eternal Father... absolve you from all the sins you have committed until this day." He told her that her sins were totally forgiven and their temporal punishment was removed as well. She was overcome with joy.

A short time later Margaret was in her little shack reflecting on the patience and kindness God had shown her after all her sins. She prayed, "Lord, how is it that you cast your eyes on me who am only dust and ashes...?" She heard the Lord say, "I went searching in the lowest depths of this world, and chose you because I wish to exalt the humble, to set sinners straight, to make noble that which is low."

She asked further, "But, why grant so many favors to such a terrible creature?"

Hope for Sinners

"Because I have chosen you to be the net of sinners. I want you to be a light to those in the darkness of habitual evil; I want the example of your conversion to preach hopefulness to those who are despairing... I want ages to come to be convinced that I am always ready to open my arms of mercy to the prodigal son who returns to me in the sincerity of his heart."

Soon after Margaret was helping a young mother in the home of a friend. She took a moment out to pray and weep over her sins. As she prayed she went into ecstasy and was lifted two or three feet off the ground. Two people were present and were amazed at what they saw. Margaret begged them not to tell anyone what they had seen. She decided then to end her work as nurse to the wealthy, believing because she was a member in the Third Order she should work among the poor instead.

The devil did not give up on Margaret after her conversion. He appeared to her as an angel of light and reminded her of her life of pleasure at Montepulciano, and how poor she was now. He warned her not to try to become so holy saying, "Better to follow the common way, as do the other Third Order members." He suggested it was enough for her to be saved, she need not strive for holiness (to which we are all called).

Margaret told him, "Be quiet," adding "The Lord has taught me the way of penance; He has promised me, if I continue on in this way, an eternal glory. My choice is made. Go away!" At that he left her.

But, he would be back. The next time he cackled and danced, sang impure songs, mixed with curse words and inviting Margaret to repeat them. She turned away. Then he appeared to her as a kind of dragon, spewing forth fire and telling her "You are damned! You are damned!" She took a burning stick from the fireplace and tried to drive him out with that, but it had no effect. Then she made the sign of the cross and he left immediately. But, as he left he threw some poison which got into her eyes and she was in pain for over an hour.

A third time he tempted her with pride, saying, "You are a saint. Everyone honors you!" She ran out of her little house and shouted out her past sins for all in the town to hear. The devil was beaten again.

At last he told her, "Your whole life is an illusion. The sweetness you have tasted is from me and not from Jesus." She began to wonder. She asked Fr. Giunta for advice and he told her to make the sign of the cross when she heard the voice which had been guiding her, and say, "If you are a spirit of darkness turned into an angel of light, be quiet and go away." Jesus then spoke to her and told her that He alone could give her such divine sweetness. At that moment light beams of truth entered her mind and she was filled with a heavenly peace. The temptations from the Satan had lasted several years.

For some time Jesus called her, "my poor little one," but she had asked Him for a more intimate title, that of daughter. He told her, "You cannot yet receive from me the sweet name of daughter, for you are the daughter of sin. When by means of another general confession you will have completely purified yourself from your sins, I will number you among my daughters."

She prayed to St. Francis of Assisi and Mary Magdalene for grace and a deeper contrition. Then she made her general confession to her priest, Fr. Giunta. It took her eight days to complete it. Then, on December 27, 1276, she received Communion wearing a rope at her throat (beneath her clothing) something a criminal would wear.

New Titles

Jesus then called her, "my daughter!" This change filled Margaret with such great delight that she feared she might die. She spent the next day in ecstasy, and from that point on she had an ever greater sorrow for her sins.

Once Our Lord said to her, "My daughter, I will place you among the Seraphs, among the virgins whose hearts are flaming with the love of God."

"How can that be," she asked, "since I have spoiled myself with so many sins?"

"My daughter, your many penances have purified your soul from all the effects of sin to such a degree that your contrition and sufferings will restore you to the purity of a virgin."

Margaret then asked Him, "...and is Mary Magdalene among the virgins in heaven?"

Jesus answered her, "Except for the Virgin Mary and Catherine the Martyr [of Alexandria] there is no one among the virgins greater than Magdalene."

Another time Jesus told her, "My daughter, you are a rose among flowers. You are pure, and for your love of chastity, I have placed you among the virgins."

Margaret prayed for the grace to "humble herself before all creatures" for the love of God. The Lord agreed, saying, "This humbling of yourself will exalt you among the blessed in heaven... You are the third light [of the Franciscan Order]" (After St. Francis, and St. Clare).

One day as she prayed, she proclaimed how unworthy she was to receive His gifts because of her evil past. "Remember," He answered, "I can give my gifts to whomever I please. Have you forgotten Mary Magdalen the sinner, the Samaritan woman, the Canaanite, Matthew the tax collector, whom I made an apostle, and the good thief, to whom I promised paradise?"

Since Father Giunta had refused her request to destroy her beauty she asked God to remove from her any graces that others might admire in her. But the Lord said to her that by these gifts "He wished to encourage sinners to be converted, and thus to contribute to His glory."

There is a lesson here for parents: if and when their daughters begin to be attractive, they should warn them of the dangers of their emerging beauty. Beauty can be a curse or a blessing. If a young woman allows herself to be drawn into the evil which godless men will propose, taken as they are by her beauty, it is a curse (as it was for Margaret in her early years). She will have many trials in life if she allows this.

But, if she gives her beauty back to God, that is, if she becomes holy through prayer and the Mass and the sacraments, and then uses her beauty to draw others to God and His own awesome beauty by speaking of the joy God has brought her in prayer, what a marvelous blessing! God (as we shall see in the "new" Margaret) will richly reward such goodness.

After raising her to the title of "my daughter," the Lord gave Margaret many other titles, including, "mother of sinners," "lily of innocence," "rose of charity," His "sister," and "pearl of his heart." However, her most treasured title was "spouse." She received this as follows: Her Guardian Angel came first and requested her consent to her marriage to the Lord. After hesitating, doubting she was worthy, she gave consent, trusting in God's will. The wedding would take place some time after.

The wedding occurred one August day within a week of the feast of the Assumption. After receiving the Eucharist in her little shack because she was sick, she received a magnificent white robe, a wedding ring and a crown from the Lord's angels. She proclaimed the words Peter had spoken, "O Jesus, You are the Christ, the Son of the living God." Then Christ answered, "And I declare, you are my spouse." To complete this marriage He placed His throne deep within her heart.

Before leaving the Lord told her, "Margaret, glorify me and I shall glorify you. Love me and I shall love you..." This "mystical marriage," is, according to St. John of the Cross, the highest spiritual state possible, in which the soul is constantly aware God's presence and love. It is this marriage with God to which we are all invited. (Isaiah 62:4, 5).

Peace Maker

In the spring of 1277 the bishop of Arezzo, who had received his title illegally, and who was a political leader first and a man of war, not peace, was about to attack Cortona. He claimed unjustly the right to rule it. Margaret heard of his plan and prayed intensely to God that her city might be spared. On May 5, 1277 the Lord appeared to her and declared, "I appoint you as peace-maker. You are to warn the bishop that he should fulfill his duties as bishop, he should let his troops go, and he should make peace with Cortona. Woe to him if he does not obey!"

Margaret was afraid to do this. After all, she was just a poor reformed sinner. But when Jesus appeared to her again on the 11th of May with more urgency, she accepted her mission and warned the bishop. It was a pleasant surprise that the bishop was convinced by Margaret's message: he made peace with Cortona in July.

Miracles

All sorts of people came to ask Margaret's prayers and many miracles occurred at her intercession. One woman came to ask Margaret's prayers for her son who had just died. After sharing in the mother's grief, Margaret told her "Go, your child is cured." She went home and found him alive and well.

Another time when parents brought their son, possessed by a devil, from another city to Margaret in Cortona, the devil left him as they approached the town. He indicated he could not stand the air filled with Margaret's prayers. When the family went on to Cortona to thank Margaret, she humbly replied, "Give credit only to God a miracle to which my sins and ingratitude could only place an obstacle."

At one point the Lord made known to her miraculously that a man in the town had just hanged himself. She and friends went immediately to his house and cut him down just in time.

Social Concerns

She showed great love for the poor, depriving herself of almost everything she had—including her coat in mid-winter, which she sent to a poor man too proud to beg—to provide for them. She said, "For my brothers the poor I would give everything, even my life, for I bear them all in my heart."

She founded a hospital in 1286, with the help of many of the important and wealthy people of Cortona. She worked there as a nurse, preferring to serve those with the most disgusting diseases. She founded a group of Third Order Franciscans in Cortona, popularly called "The Little Poor Sisters," to serve at the hospital. They were approved by bishop Ubertini on May 26, 1286. Margaret herself wrote the Rule.

She founded another group, the confraternity of Our Lady of Mercy, to not only provide for the material needs of the hospital, but also serve the City's poor, especially those too shy to ask. They were to take particular care of the Franciscans when ill; and, in time of civil war, they were to band together to promote peace. The Blessed Mother was to be their guide, and they were to seek the good of all, without seeking any recognition for themselves.

As a mother, Margaret was careful never to spoil her son, but to raise him with loving discipline. She first cooked with great care the food for the poor, and only when they had been served would she provide for her son, and his meal was uncooked. When he entered the Franciscans in 1283, she wrote to him urging him, among other things, to strive always for humility, to pray with great zeal, and to control his "sensual appetites," so as to give his heart entirely to God.

Shortly after entering, one morning the young man overslept and missed the start of prayer. The superior had to wake him up by tapping him with a stick. The boy woke all of a sudden and instinctively grabbed the stick and broke it. Then, realizing what he had done, he asked forgiveness and slapped his own face. Margaret somehow knew and sent him a message to come to her. When he arrived she scolded him for his failure to be at prayer promptly. He accepted her correction well.

The Cross

On one Good Friday Margaret was given visions of the Passion of our Lord. People gathered around her in the church as she seemed to experience every pain of Jesus, her arms outstretched as if on the cross herself. At 3:00 pm she seemed to almost die. The people in the church cried uncontrollably. When she came to her senses, she gave thanks to God for this privilege. However, when she saw all the people gathered around her she was disappointed that so many had seen this precious moment she shared with the Lord.

Nonetheless, the Lord said to her, "Relax, my daughter, I want you to be the mirror of sinners, even the most stubborn. I want them to be convinced by your example that my merciful heart is always open to those who repent."

"Lord, when your glory and the salvation of souls are at stake, I joyfully submit."

On Easter she was moved by the Spirit to ask Fr. Giunta as he was preaching, "Do you know where my Savior is, my crucified Jesus?" echoing the words of Mary Magdalene. "Console yourself," he answered, "...He will not be slow to show Himself to you." The next day Jesus appeared to her in His glorified body, filling her with peace and tremendous joy.

Nobles, poor people, priests came from all over, Rome, Florence, but not just Italy; they came from France and Spain as well to see Margaret and ask for her prayers and advice. Fr. Giunta was swamped with the many people who wanted to go to confession after they visited with her.

She asked her guardian angel once, "...let me know by what signs I can distinguish the true friends of God, that is to say, the elect."

Her angel responded, "He is one of the elect whose heart is detached from every unreasonable earthly desire, is united to its Creator, tends without ceasing toward Him and sighs only for Him.

"But," continued Margaret, "what virtues should he possess?"

"...the following three virtues: a deep humility, like that of Jesus crucified; perfect charity; extreme purity of heart. He who denies himself, crucifies himself, not with nails but with the denial of self will, and is willing to suffer, to shed his blood if necessary, to proclaim his faith. He... has compassion with the sufferings of the poor, hates falsehood, and flies with horror from impurity. Finally, he takes upon himself the pains of others, and is saddened or rejoices with them without ever yielding to envy."

Margaret sometimes expressed sadness when Jesus did not appear to her. He appeared to her after that and told her, "Margaret, you want heaven here on earth. Bear in mind that this cannot be. Life on earth is for hard work and temptation; and if at times I give you the consolation of my presence, you must not forget that you must also at times walk in darkness and suffer."

Another time Jesus spoke to Margaret as follows: "My child, why do you seek to find a paradise here on earth when I denied it to my own body, united though it was to my Divinity? You must not hope for this for in no way can it be given you. You are like Peter, who having seen my glory on Mt. Tabor, wanted in the [delight] of his soul to build there three tents and to live there because of the sweetness which filled his soul. And, as his desire was not fulfilled, so neither can you possess here on earth the paradise I have promised you in the life to come."

Jesus appeared to her once with His crown of thorns, and holes in his hands and feet as he appeared on Good Friday. Margaret called out, "Ah., Lord, let me be crucified with You!." Jesus replied, "Yes, you shall be martyred with Me... But it is not your flesh but your heart which shall be crucified." Then He gave her a vision of an old shack on a nearby hill and told her she was to live there alone.

Despite the protests of her fellow religious and the Franciscans, on May 1, 1288, Margaret climbed the hill with a friend and moved into that miserable house. There, the Lord appeared to her and urged her, "Go, be the angel of peace and the apostle of my mercies. I want you to preach peace to the people of Cortona. Warn them that if they do not do penance, the arm of my justice will rest heavily upon them." He also told her to have Fr. Giunta preach the need for peace in Cortona and that He would be with him. Margaret felt unworthy of her mission but was totally obedient. She went out and shouted in the streets, "People of Cortona, do penance and make peace with your enemies."

The people responded magnificently. Alas, when she also warned Bishop Ubertini not to carry out his plans to wage war on Florence, he ignored her and went to war. He was killed, his army destroyed, and his body hung from the arch of a church in Florence.

Shortly after she moved to her mountain home Margaret began to suffer a great deal. Her consolations were taken away, she had no one to speak to most of the time, her miracles ended as did her prophecies.

People began to be critical of her and ridicule her. Some were upset that the Franciscans spent so much effort to guide such a sinner. Others claimed she practiced witchcraft or was mentally ill, or was possessed.

One woman came to see her and reminded her harshly of her former sins, and accused her of hypocrisy. Margaret responded by praying for her, asking God to forgive her, and doing what she could to help her. Indeed, she prayed for *all* her critics, and forgave them in her heart. She said, "The insults I endure for the love of God seem sweeter to me than honey, and pour more delight into my soul than all consolations." She prayed to God, "Forgive them all, Lord... If you need a victim, Lord, take me. Let the blows of your justice fall on my head, but let theirs be spared."

The Franciscans themselves were divided as to Margaret's spiritual state. Fr. Giunta stood up for her, but others believed she had fooled him. The case of Margaret was brought up at the Provincial Chapter in 1288, and although the new Provincial was a believer in Margaret's holiness, to avoid criticism, he decided to limit Fr. Giunta's contact with her to once every eight days.

Two years later another leader was elected, who re-assigned Fr. Giunta to Siena, so Margaret was completely deprived of her spiritual guide. Two others took his place, but Margaret was broken-hearted.

Margaret began to feel terrible dryness in prayer, as if God were not even hearing her. She begged God to show Himself to her again, but he remained hidden. For almost a year this went on, and then finally Jesus spoke to her. She asked Him, "Why have you abandoned me so long?"

Jesus answered, "I have not abandoned you. I am always near you, but you want to nourish yourself on the milk of consolations and it is necessary, that being the daughter of my Heart, you should be drenched with gall along with me." He told her that her continuing to pray when everything seemed so dry gave Him more honor and benefitted her more since she served Him, as He said, "not according to your taste but according to mine. Earth is a place of combat and I do not want you to taste there the delights of Paradise."

"Ah, Lord," she answered, "Where you are, there is Paradise." After this appearance of the Lord, Margaret had the joy and peace of being always in God's presence, even while experiencing the trials which so often come with that intimacy. She lived the life of a contemplative, pouring out her heart in prayer and penance in her mountain retreat, far from the company of others.

It is said that she imitated there the prayer and penance that St. Mary Magdalene offered during the final 30 years of her life in a cave in Provence (France). One July 21, the evening before the saint's feast day, the Lord appeared to her with Mary Magdalene and said to Margaret, "See the one whom I pardoned in the house of the Pharisee? That silvery robe which covers her shoulders, those diamonds which sparkle in her crown, behold the price of her penance in the cave."

At one point Jesus appeared to Margaret and told her, "All that you ask of the Father in my name you will obtain. "Cortona," He said, "Deserved to be punished, but due to the love and honor it gives to you, I will spare it..."

The Holy Eucharist

Margaret had a great love for the Eucharist, and loved to "run to the source of Divine love," as she put it, that is, the tabernacle. After her conversion she received Communion often and when she entered the Third Order, she had been given permission by Fr. Giunta to receive every day, an unusual privilege for that time. She would arrive at church at 6 am and spent two or three hours in prayer before Mass. She spent a long time after Communion in near ecstasy, giving thanks for the great Gift she had received.

Once as she was approaching communion she stopped as she felt she might be unworthy. She prayed to God for guidance and heard Jesus within her say, "Pure are the rays which the sun sends to the earth; purer still should be the soul which receives Communion." He then expressed sadness about the lack of reverence toward Him among some people, but then reassured Margaret that He "delighted to dwell" within her. "Receive Communion without fear," He told her.

It was after communion that Jesus spoke to her most intimately and that she experienced the delightful ecstasies. It was then that Jesus gave her His most wonderful gifts and great insights into His Divinity.

She once told her spiritual director, Fr. Giunta, "With the strength I receive [at the tabernacle] nothing would stop me [from martyrdom] and I would count as nothing the most terrible tortures. What should I not do for love of my Jesus?"

Death

In late 1296 Fr. Giunta returned to Cortona from Siena, where he had been sent in 1290. She had predicted he would return before her death. Her health had already begun to fail: she had rheumatism and suffered a constant fever.

On January 3, 1297 an angel appeared to her and told her, "...on the 22nd of February, at the first glimpse of dawn, you shall fly toward the home of the saved, where the mercy of God has reserved for you a place of honor." Margaret was filled with joy at the thought.

When she later doubted that God could honor her after her former life of sin, Jesus appeared to her and told her "Be reassured, it is your good guardian angel who has spoken to you, and what he told you will be fulfilled. The exalted Virgin Mary, St Francis, St Mary

Magdalen and the whole heavenly court call upon me to hasten the day of your entry into Paradise, and I have resolved to hear them." She was overjoyed at this news. The devil tried to tempt her one last time, but her friends comforted her and Fr. Giunta brought her communion every day.

For the final 17 days of her life her only food was the Holy Eucharist. Everyone in the town wanted to come to visit this holy woman as she lay on her death bed, and scores of people had the privilege. She spoke kind words of encouragement to each with the sweetest smile.

On the evening of February 21 Fr. Giunta anointed her. She said tender goodbyes to her fellow Franciscans and asked forgiveness for the shameful sins of her youth, and urged them to bless God with her for His infinite mercy. Before dawn the next day the holy priest brought her Viaticum. As the first rays of dawn appeared she passed from this life, eager to join her beloved Lord in the eternal marriage of His Kingdom.

At the very time of her death a holy monk who lived in Castello was given a vision of her soul rising up to heaven as a sphere of fire, accompanied by a number of souls who had been set free from Purgatory by the merits of her sufferings. The monk called out to her "The New Magdalen." It was February 22, 1297. She was 50 years old.

Almost immediately miracles began to occur at her tomb,

including the raising to life of twelve persons when people prayed for them there. More than a hundred people were cured when they prayed to her.

Her own body remains incorrupt, that is, whole and without decay to this day, and can be seen beneath the main altar of the Basilica of Cortona, "St. Margaret's," named in her honor. She was canonized in 1728.

Reflection

Margaret of Cortona fell into the sad pattern of the beautiful girl who never got the love she needed at home. So, she sought it outside home and was willing to sin to keep it. She misused her gift and found misery.

But, by the mercy of God, she was given the chance to start over. She took back her gift from the world and gave it to God. He had a better use for it, a noble one: to save souls. This brought her happiness, true, lasting happiness.

But, even after her conversion, Margaret had an important lesson to learn, one that Jesus Himself taught her: You can't find heaven on earth. Although we receive tastes of heaven here, as Peter, James and John did at the Transfiguration, we must "also at times walk in darkness and suffer." Why? Because we share in the mission of Christ, to make reparation for the sins of the world. Once we resign ourselves to that truth, we will understand life so much better.

Margaret is truly a saint for today. Her life dramatically illustrates the power of God's inexhaustible mercy. Our sins—be they sexual promiscuity, homosexuality, drug or alcohol abuse, or even abortion—leave their permanent scars on our hearts, our minds and even our bodies. But the blood of Christ can wipe clean our *souls* so that no scar, no trace of sin remains.

With our persevering love and repentance Christ can raise us from the depths of sin to the heights of holiness, as he raised Margaret and others such as St. Augustine and St. Mary Magdalene. Best to be sinless and deeply loving as our Blessed Mother was, but better to be a repentant sinner who loves much than one who has sinned little but loves little. "Love covers a multitude of sins" (1 Peter 4:8).

Sources

Léopold, de Chérancé, *Saint Margaret of Cortona*, English trans. by R. F. O'Connor, NY: Benziger Brothers, 1903, pp. 12-215

Cuthbert, Father, OFM Cap., *A Tuscan Penitent*, Chicago: Benziger Brothers, 1907, pp. 39-193.

Alban Goodier, S. J., *Saints for Sinners*, New York: Doubleday, 1959, pp. 34-43.

Hiral, Most Rev. Ange-Marie Hiral, OFM, *The Revelations of Margaret of Cortona*, English trans. Raphael Brown, Franciscan Inst., 1952 pp. 2-64.

Thurston, Herbert J., S. J., and Attwater, Donald, *Butler's Lives of the Saints*, Volume I, Westminster, MD: Christian Classics, 1981, pp. 396-398.

Chapter Three

St. Augustine of Hippo

(354-430)

St. Augustine is perhaps one of the most colorful saints the Catholic Church has ever known. By the first 30 years of his life it seemed he would be one of the world's worst sinners, but through the prayers of his mother and his own love for the truth, and the influence of St. Ambrose, he became one of its great saints.

Youth

St. Augustine was born November 13, 354 at Tagaste in North Africa (today, Souk Ahras, Algeria) to Patricius and Monica. His father was a pagan, with a violent temper, but through the efforts of his holy wife, St. Monica, became a Catholic just before his death. Augustine described his father as poor, but they had servants and owned some land so they were not so poor by our standards.

Monica taught Augustine the faith when he was young but (as many foolish people of the time did) he delayed Baptism for fear of sinning after. He was a lazy student, disobedient to his parents and teachers, studying only to avoid being beaten, which he feared. He wasn't slow; he just liked to play.

Life of Sin

At 16, he fell into sins of lust, with no religious convictions to hold him back. He competed with his friends to accomplish more and more sexual sins.

That same year he moved to Carthage (known as a "sin city" of his time), where he eagerly studied rhetoric and with great success, adding to his already considerable pride. Within a year he moved in with a girlfriend, with whom he lived, unmarried, for the next 14 years. They had a son, Adeodatus, in 372. At the time he was behaving better than many of the men in Carthage, in that he had only one woman and did not go out seeking others. Even the married men of the time were often out at night with other women! However, he himself admitted the huge difference between such a "bargain of lustful love" and a true marriage.

Erroneous Beliefs

Augustine was attracted to philosophy and the Bible, but, because of his pride, as he said, he didn't get very far understanding the Bible. Of his search for the truth, he later wrote, "I sought with pride what only humility could make me find... and I fell to the ground."

He was more impressed in the style of Cicero's philosophy than the truth of the Bible. He became a Manichean, tying to understand why there was evil in the world. The Manichees held that God was the cause of spirit, which was good, but matter was evil. This heresy, called dualism, is contrary to the Church's teaching that both matter and spirit are caused by God, and thus are good, although the spirit is more important than matter.

The Manicheans promised to lead him to truth, but they were better at tearing down the Catholic faith than in defending the truth of their own. He wanted to arrive at knowledge rather than faith, thinking the two were opposed to each other. He found it difficult to accept that God had become man in Jesus, since the flesh, as something evil, would have dragged down His divinity. Later he realized that faith is necessary to get at certain truths which our human reason cannot discover without help, and that the flesh, as God's creation, is good. When he argued about religion with uneducated Christians, he nearly always won, even when he was wrong!

Nonetheless, Augustine had some serious questions about the Manichean religion, which no one around him could answer. When the Manichean leader, Faustus, came to Carthage in 383, Augustine fired away with his questions. Although Faustus was pleasant and spoke well, without pride, he side-stepped Augustine's questions. In time Augustine came to realize that Manicheanism was not a valid religion as he had hoped, but he saw nowhere else to go, so he continued on with it until he could find something else.

Secretly to Rome

A bit later in 383, Augustine decided to leave Carthage and travel to Rome. He had run his own schools in Carthage and Tagaste for nine years, but heard that the Roman students were far better behaved than those in Carthage. He was tired of unregistered students bursting into his classroom and noisy students disrupting the order of his classes.

However, before he could leave, he had to deal with one major obstacle–his mother Monica. He feared she might try to keep him from going or she might try to go with him to Rome. So, he pretended he was seeing off a friend from the dock. Although she went there with him, he told her the lie that he had to wait there until a good sailing wind came up to see off his friend. He arranged for her to spend the night in a nearby church, where she prayed in tears that her son would not leave her. God refused her that prayer that He might, as Augustine later wrote, arrange to answer her greatest prayer–his conversion.

So, off he sailed. When she discovered his trick Monica was broken-hearted. She wiped up her tears and returned home to Tagaste.

At Rome Augustine became very ill, near death in fact. He wrote in his autobiography, *The Confessions*, that had he died at that time, he would have gone to hell for his sins. While he was sick he stayed with some Manicheans and he saw first hand how this religion just didn't work. His host, who was wealthy, tried to gather a number Manicheans to live in community with him, but very quickly there were all sorts of conflicts and the whole thing fell apart. This convinced Augustine that he was finished with Manicheanism.

Having rejected Manicheanism and Christianity, Augustine did not know where to turn. He began to wonder if it was even possible to discover the truth about life and especially about God. Yet, he could not completely give up his desire to find the truth.

Meanwhile he threw himself into his work at Rome, to teach rhetoric. Alas, he discovered rather quickly that Roman students would stay with a teacher until payment was due, and then go together to another teacher. In this way they would avoid having to pay for their studies. So, he applied for a teaching job in Milan and was accepted.

Milan and Ambrose

Once in Milan (in 384), he met (St.) Ambrose, the bishop there, who was famous for his preaching and his holiness. He welcomed Augustine warmly, "in a fatherly fashion" as Augustine put it. The young teacher began to come to church to listen to Ambrose preach, not to believe in his words, in which he had no interest, but to observe his speaking skills. Nonetheless, he gradually began to be attracted by his words as well.

Shortly after Augustine arrived in Milan, his mother followed him there. (When someone got a good job it was customary for friends and family members to come and live with the person.)

He told his mother he had abandoned the Manichean faith, but had not embraced Christianity. Augustine continued to attend Ambrose's sermons, but was not ready to commit to this faith the bishop explained so well. In 386 the Emperor's mother, Justina, asked Ambrose for the Porcian basilica so it could be used by the heretical Arian bishop. Ambrose could not do that in good conscience so he flatly refused her and knowing there would be trouble, he entered the basilica with other bishops and good Catholics, including Monica, and locked the doors, barricading themselves in. They sang hymns there, and prayed for protection from the emperor. The emperor's troops surrounded the building, but Ambrose held out. Finally he won when the troops left on Good Friday, 386 and Justina gave up her plans. Augustine was deeply moved by this event.

He was also impressed (somewhat) by the events surrounding the moving of two martyrs' bodies. These bodies were found to be incorrupt and some miracles occurred, including the healing of a blind man. All this had the effect of calming the anger of Justina, and kindling a spark of faith in Augustine, though just a small one.

Nearing Conversion

He again took up the writings of St. Paul and this time, because his heart was more open, he was able to understand what he could not previously. In the Scriptures he found something he had not found in any other religion or philosophy: humility. He found humility only in Christ.

With the help of Ambrose and Monica Augustine gradually began to see the errors of his ways and appeared on the verge of conversion. He agreed to send home his live-in girlfriend—with great sorrow—and marry a Christian girl. It seems he could not marry his mistress by law because of social status. Monica found him a young woman to marry, and he was happy with the choice. However, since the girl was too young to give legal consent, a two-year delay was necessary. Augustine couldn't wait: alas, he took another woman to live with him to tide him over.

At this point he was ready to embrace the Catholic faith in his mind but he was bound by a kind of slavery to lust which he struggled to overcome. As a young man he had prayed for chastity: "Give me chastity and self-control, but not yet." It seems he waited too long, as now that he wanted to surrender to God and His Gospel, he was addicted to sex. He was, as he put it, "overwhelmed with shame and horror..."

At about this time an African Christian by the name of Ponticianus came to visit Augustine. When he saw the writings of St. Paul on Augustine's table, he began to speak of St. Antony of the Desert who had founded a number of monasteries in Egypt. He told of two soldiers who read about St. Antony and began to ask themselves why they were giving their lives to this world when they could become friends with God by doing as St. Antony had done. They were so inspired that they left their fiancées and joined a monastery near Milan, headed by Ambrose. The women they were engaged to entered convents. Augustine was amazed to hear of this conversion and was ashamed of his own delay in converting.

He went into a nearby garden with his friend Alypius and wrestled with himself over his delay in surrendering to God and His truth. He thought of his former lovers who seemed to tempt him, "Do you think you can live without [these sins]?" On the other hand he saw in his mind one who might be called "Lady Chastity" who seemed to show him all sorts of people, young and old, who had been given the gift of chastity by our Lord. He felt she was urging him to trust himself to God, and be healed.

Tormented by his struggle, he went apart from Alypius and began to weep bitter tears. He cried out "How long, how long? Why not now... an end to my uncleanness?"

Take and Read

As he said these things, he heard the voice of a child calling out, "Take and read, take and read." He took that as a message from God inviting him to pick up the Bible and read whatever page he opened to. He opened to Romans and read, "let us conduct ourselves rightly... not in reveling and drunkenness, not in debauchery and licentiousness, not in quarreling and jealousy. But put on the Lord Jesus Christ, and make no provision for the flesh, to gratify its desires" (Rom. 13:13, 14). That was his answer. He must surrender to God and delay no more.

He told Alypius what had happened, and Alypius took the book from which Augustine was reading and read the next sentence, "As for the man who is weak in faith, welcome him..." (Rom 14:1). He saw that as referring to himself, and he resolved to convert as well.

The two went to tell Monica and she was delighted. She was even more thrilled that he had decided to give up worldly success and having a wife, and to give himself entirely to God. The year was 386. Augustine was 31.

He completed his teaching term in late August and gave up his teaching position. He moved to a quiet house in the country, provided by a friend, to prepare for his baptism. With him went his mother, his son, his brother, Alypius and six others. They began to have intense discussions about philosophy and theology.

Augustine prayed a great deal each morning and stayed up to meditate half the night, often weeping for his past sins. He fasted as well.

He returned to Milan in March to register for baptism, and to take the preparatory classes. He attended Mass there and came to love the hymns they sang, which often brought tears to his eyes. Later he would write, "Singing is for one who loves."

Baptism

Augustine was baptized by Ambrose at the Easter Vigil Mass, April 24, 387. He was 32. Augustine finally experienced the rest, of which he later wrote, "... [Lord], you have made us for yourself, and our heart is restless until it rests in you."

His study did not stop with his Baptism, but before long he began to think about returning to Tagaste. This would be a good place for the small group, all from there, to continue their kind of monastic life of study. Augustine had inherited his father's land holdings, which included a country house.

So they set out to return home in late summer, 387. They reached Ostia, from where they would sail to Africa. There, while resting from their travel from Milan, his mother Monica died. She was 55.

Return to Tagaste

The rest of the group, after returning to Rome for several months, set out for Tagaste. There he set up a kind of monastery, where they lived as poor men, prayed much, fasted, studied and served others by their works.

Alas, although they were happy to be home, Augustine's reputation preceded him so many of the townspeople sought his attention that he did not have the leisure time to study and pray as he wanted. After staying there three years, he and his friends began to think of starting a kind of monastery in another city so they could have the peace and quiet they sought.

By this time people around Africa had come to know his story and his strong devotion, and many wanted him to be their bishop. Because of that he stayed far from places where the bishop had recently died and the people were awaiting a new one. The place they chose was Hippo, near the ocean, which had a good, healthy bishop.

However, the bishop was looking for a priest to help him, and only a short time after Augustine and his friends had arrived, announced this at Mass one Sunday. The people saw Augustine there, got hold of him and brought him to the bishop. Augustine resisted with cries and tears, but they would not be denied. He gave in, and shortly thereafter the bishop ordained him a priest.

He had resisted because he wanted to live a monastic life with his friends, and he thought the priesthood was a huge responsibility. He thought it beyond his strength. So, once he was chosen he began to prepare himself for this office. He asked to have more time to prepare and this was given.

He was ordained in 391. Once ordained, he asked the bishop for a place to establish another monastery, and the bishop gave him a place to do that. With him were his long-time friends, St. Alipius, St. Evodius, St. Possidius among others. He began bringing together other men who wanted to devote themselves to God and to own nothing, as Augustine did. (He had sold his property in Tagaste.) Everything would be owned by the group in common, and each would be given what he needed from that.

This way of serving God began to be copied throughout Africa. Not surprisingly, very holy and educated priests and bishops came from this movement. The Church in Africa underwent a great renewal, a badly needed one.

Opposing Errors

Augustine was ready to fight for the faith against every error being proposed, and there were plenty of errors around in his time. In 392 A Manichean priest named Fortunatus was gaining a number of converts so the people asked Augustine to debate him. Augustine agreed and Fortunatus reluctantly agreed as well. The debate went on for two days. Finally, Fortunatus admitted he had no answers for Augustine's arguments and the debate ended. Fortunatus left Hippo and many were converted to the Catholic faith.

Augustine wrote in a bold, manly way and we might think he was a tall, hardy, dashing young man. Not so. He was short, "thin, stooped and already graying" in his mid-forties. He had a long beard. His asthma often caused him difficulty breathing and kept him from sleeping many nights. But none of that kept him from being an energetic defender of the Catholic faith.

After a short while, bishop Valerius realized that a neighboring diocese might try to kidnap Augustine and make him their bishop, something which had been tried but had failed. His friends from the monastery, Alypius and Profuturus had already been requested and ordained bishops in other dioceses. So, Valerius tried to arrange to have Augustine ordained bishop, and be his successor. Augustine resisted. Also the consecrating bishop, Megalius, was against it since he believed the false rumor that Augustine had been casting love-spells.

Bishop

So, Valerius devised a sneaky plan to accomplish his goal. He invited Megalius and other bishops to visit Hippo during a regional bishops' conference, and announced his intention with all in attendance. All the people let out great cries of approval. Augustine gave in and Megalius discovered the rumor to be a lie, so the ordination of Augustine took place in 395. When Valerius died shortly thereafter, Augustine became the bishop of Hippo.

Augustine was not about to be an arrogant, proud leader. He called himself "A servant of Christ, and, in His name, a servant of his servants." His motto was, "To rule is to serve." He always said he would rather be in a monastery, where he could spend more time praying or studying the Bible, but he concluded, "We are servants of the Church, and servants above all, of its weakest members." He said at one point to his people, "I am fearful at what I am for you, but I draw strength from what I am with you. I am a bishop for you, a Christian with you." He urged them to pray for him.

He remarked once that the way to God was first, humility, second, humility, and third, humility. "Not that there are no other precepts to give, but if humility does not precede all that we do, our efforts are fruitless." His own claim to this virtue was exemplified in a letter to St. Jerome in which he wrote: "I urge you again and again to correct me confidently when you see I need it; for though the office of bishop [Augustine] is greater than that of a priest [Jerome], yet in many ways Augustine is inferior to Jerome."

When he became bishop he wanted to establish another monastery, but as a bishop he had to have a house where people could stay when visiting. This would disrupt a monastery of laymen as he had established in the past. So, he began a house for clerics–priests, deacons, etc. to live in community, owning nothing. The apostolic life in Jerusalem was the pattern they followed.

According to his biographer, St. Possidius, the clothes and furniture were neat and clean but simple. The food was simple, but meat was provided rarely for guests and the sick, as was wine in moderation. The occasional use of wine and meat was in part to show to the Manicheans around that such things were good, not evil. Augustine had no use for gossip, and actually had a sign up in the dining room which read,

Who injures the name of an absent friend
May not at this table as guest attend.

When some close bishop friends became critical of some others, Augustine insisted they stop, and threatened to leave the table in the middle of the meal if they did not. Because of the dangers of such conversation, he had the custom of having some spiritual reading or discussion at the dinner table.

One of the rules stated, "It is better to have fewer needs rather than more things." By possessing less, they were able to give more to the needy. And, they gave much to the poor, using church income or even at times selling sacred items to ransom captives. He began the annual tradition of providing clothes for all the needy in each parish.

Preaching

Augustine preached each morning, but at times he had to preach twice, or even more in a day. This, in spite of his weak health and frail voice. In fact, he had to stop at times out of exhaustion or his voice giving out. He found preaching very wearing, but he continued on, seeing it as his duty. He was often invited to preach in other churches throughout Africa. For a bishop to preach this much was most unusual.

He would always pray before preaching and even asked the congregation beforehand to pray that he might serve them well in speaking. He spoke in familiar terms, often using informal expressions which might be used in the street, so as to be sure he was understood.

He seldom wrote out his homilies before hand, and so he would sometimes start on one subject and end on another. There were often people in the congregation to write down his words and thus we have many of his sermons today. All had to stand at Mass, on the dirt floor, with the men and women separated by the middle aisle. The people would respond aloud to the preacher, sometimes clapping when they liked his words. Augustine loved this interaction, and would always speak very directly, very personally to each person, making contact with their eyes.

At times he would tell a somewhat crude joke. And when the

aroma of the congregation became strong (in those pre-deodorant days), he quipped, "I can tell by the smell that I must have spoken [too long] today." He told stories and referred often to the current situation in Africa. He used rich examples, as for example he once said, "The perverse Donatists are like [donkeys] and horses which kick the people who are trying to cure their ills."

Sometimes when they cheered him on by applause he would say loudly, "I want your good behavior, not your applause!" At other times he was stronger, "I don't want the praise of those living evil lives–in fact I detest it... You applaud me but I ask myself: what kind of lives are these people living who now praise me?" He knew the danger of praise, knowing it could lead to pride, yet he did not completely reject it lest he be ungrateful. He wanted to be saved, but not without his people.

Opposing More Heresies

As bishop, Augustine had even more work to do against heretics. He wrote a work showing the errors of the Manichean "catechism," and a longer work against the Manichean bishop Faustus' book criticizing the Catholic faith. When he received a letter from Mani-chean Secundius, urging him to come back to the Manichean religion and criticizing the Catholic faith, Augustine wrote back, carefully showing the errors of Manicheaism. When a Manichean named Felix came to Hippo in 404 to win converts, Augustine challenged him to either answer publicly the questions Fortunatus couldn't answer before or leave the city. He agreed and after the second debate, admitted defeat. Shortly thereafter he joined the Catholic Church.

The Donatists

The Donatists were another heretical group he had to deal with. They believed that the validity of a sacrament was dependent on the moral uprightness of the person administering it. In fact, the Church teaches that a sacrament is valid if the minister intends to do what the Church does. The Church recognizes baptism performed by anyone, even a non-Christian if they fulfill that condition. And, in Hippo the Donatists were in the majority, having many more members than the Catholics. In some nearby towns there were no Catholics left–all were Donatists.

One of the first things he did was to write a song with rhyming stanzas which explained the history of Donatism and why it was wrong. After this he wrote several books disputing the Donatists. He invited the Donatist bishop of Hippo to discuss the faith with him, but the bishop refused. And, so did other nearby bishops whom he invited.

In 401 a meeting of Catholic bishops was held in Africa about the Donatist problem. At the meeting Augustine, with his typical kindness, backed a statement that Donatist bishops, priests and deacons should be welcomed back into the Church with their same rank should they decide to return to Catholicism.

Based on their discussions many priests and bishops went out with a clear explanation of how the Donatists had split off from true Catholicism. However, a group of violent Donatists called Circum-cellions began to go around in gangs and persecute Catholic leaders. They attacked priests and other Church people day and night, stole their goods, tortured them and even broke the legs of some, crippling them. Others they blinded by throwing acid in their eyes, and some they even killed. Even some Donatists shunned these criminals.

Once they prepared to ambush Augustine, to rid themselves of their most effective enemy, as he traveled to another town to speak. On the way he took a wrong turn and arrived by a different route, thus thwarting the plan of the Circumcellions. It wasn't until later that he discovered his providential deliverance from great harm. When he did, he and all his companions gave thanks to God.

Because of the Circumcellions, Augustine was persuaded at the Council of Carthage in 404 to ask for the emperor's protection. And so the emperor issued a law banning Donatist religious services, exiling their priests and bishops, and even threatening execution.

In time the Donatists appealed to the Emperor and a public meeting was called in 411 at Carthage to hear their side of things. At that meeting, in the presence of the Emperor's ambassador, there were

286 Catholic bishops and 284 Donatist bishops. Before the debate began, Augustine invited the Catholic bishops to be willing to give up their dioceses to the Donatists should they lose the debate and 28 of the 30 bishops he asked agreed.

During the meeting Augustine patiently endured the "delaying tactics" of the Donatists and clearly showed the origin of the controversy; he urged prayer, alms and fasting for unity between the two groups. The Donatists tried to spread all sorts of harmful false rumors about Augustine, that he was a meddler, that he might still be a Manichean, that he was involved with women as he had been in the past. Augustine knew they were trying to derail the conference by tearing him down, so he strongly defended himself and clearly showed that the Donatists had caused the split some hundred years before.

The Emperor's representative became convinced that the cause of all the public disturbances was due to the Donatist insistence on their errors. As a result, the Emperor renewed the ban of the Donatists in 412 (and in 414 and 428) and under such strong legal penalties, the Donatists began to fade away.

From 412 to 421 Augustine wrote several books showing how wrong Donatism was. Also during this time he went to Caesarea in Mauritania when asked by the pope, to debate the Donatist bishop there. This completed Augustine's 30-year conflict with the Donatist heresy. Although it continued in certain areas, he had effectively won the battle.

This great bishop proclaimed the Church a mother, who invites her children in tears. He wrote in his song against the Donatists, "Why do you abandon me, and why must I be tormented by your final death?" He preached, "Outside the Church you can have everything–except salvation." Having lived much of his life outside it, he *loved* the Church.

Pelagianism

Augustine faced another terrible error in his time, that of Pelagianism. Its originator, Pelagius, held that Original Sin was not passed on to others beyond Adam, and that newborn infants were in the state of grace, and thus did not need baptism. He also held that there were sinless people before the coming of Christ. Augustine wrote a book against Pelagian ideas at the request of Marcellinus, the pope's representative, and went to Carthage and elsewhere to preach against these errors. In addition, he wrote several other books showing how Pelagianism was wrong.

In his book, *On The Punishment and Remission of Sin*, he made it clear that every decision to do what is good is preceded by a grace from God. This he based on St. Paul's statement, "What have you that you did not receive? If then you received it, why do you boast as if it were not a gift?" Pelagius was condemned by two African councils in 416 and by Pope Innocent in 417. However, Innocent's successor,

Pope Zosimus, was tricked into reversing Innocent's condemnation the same year.

Seeing the error, Augustine immediately wrote strongly to Zosimus asking him to continue the condemnation of Pelagius. The African bishops repeated their condemnation of Pelagianism in 417, proclaiming that God's grace enables us to know what is good, and also to do it. That grace precedes every good act or word.

Unfortunately, Zosimus replied that he was going to leave things as they were. So, Augustine wrote to the Emperor, Honorius. He did act in 418, expelling Pelagius and his disciple Celestius from Rome and declaring that their followers were to lose their possessions and be sent away as well. After this Pope Zosimus too condemned Pelagius and Celestius.

Throughout all these conflicts with heretics, Augustine tried always to show love for his opponents. He wrote, "Let them say what they want against us; for our part let us love them even if they do not want our love."

Sometimes the arguments that flew back and forth became very strong. When Julian, the wordy Pelagian insulted Augustine's mother, the bishop wrote him back,

You have insulted even the memory of my mother, a woman who never did you any harm... A sure sign, is it not, that you have succumbed to the evil spirit of slander? Have you no fear of the Scriptures?: "Slanderers shall not possess the kingdom of God." ...For my part, I think your parents, Catholic Christians, are to be honored, and I am happy for them that they died before seeing you become a heretic.

Confessions

Augustine's greatest work was his autobiography, *Confessions*, which he wrote between 397 and 400. Therein he described how he had lived an evil life, and eventually found his way to God. In it he wrote one of the most beautiful paragraphs ever written on conversion:

> Late have I loved you, O Beauty so ancient and so new... I rushed headlong after these things of beauty which you have made... They kept me far from you, those fair things which, were they not in you, would not exist at all... You have sent forth fragrance, and I have drawn in my breath, and I pant for you. I have tasted you, and I hunger and thirst for you. You have touched me and I have burned for your peace.[1]

He loved beauty and saw God as the source of all beauty–and

_____

[1]Adapted from *The Confessions of St. Augustine*, trans. by John K. Ryan, Garden City, NY: Image Books (Doubleday), 1960, pp. 254, 255}

goodness. The greatest beauty on this earth he found in persons. (In fact the most beautiful persons on earth could be said to be symbols of the unsurpassed beauty of God.)

Regarding love, he proclaimed, "The measure for loving God is God Himself. The measure for this love is to love without measure."

Augustine, at the age of 56, looked older than his age due to many sleepless nights caused by asthma and almost constant work. His skin was dark, his hair and beard white, and his voice worn out. He refused to dress any better than his priests.

Barbarian Invasions

In 410 the Visigoth Alaric marched into Rome with his army and conquered the great city (it was his 3rd attempt), and just about destroyed it. They burned property and tortured and killed many. This horrible scene of dead bodies and burned out buildings seemed to symbolize the end of Roman glory.

Augustine was broken-hearted over the fall of Rome, the center of the Christian faith and culture. He saw this as an end of Roman civilization and a fall into a world of barbarism where violence and cruelty would rule, rather than decency and law. Romans came pouring into Africa and Augustine insisted his people welcome them and care for them as their brothers and sisters.

A friend even suggested to Augustine that the fall of Rome

signaled that the end of world was near. Augustine wrote back saying he doubted the end was near, and, "Rome is not lost if the Romans are not lost." He knew that if people thought the end was near they would do little to help the pitiable Romans who were in such need.

The Pagans began to blame the fall of Rome on the Christians, claiming that when people worshiped pagan gods, all was well. Augustine replied in his book, the *City of God* that the horror inflicted by the Goths was due to the excessive concern of Christians for the things of this world. And too, there had been many crises in Rome in pagan times. He went on to criticize with sometimes "violent" words the pagan sacrifices, in which millions of animals were slain in their temples, and in which the pagan priests sometimes would tear out the inner organs and try to read a prophecy from them.

In his book, which took him more than ten years to finish, he contrasts the two "cities," that of God, and the "Earthly City," that of Satan. The first is founded on the love of God, the second, on the love of self. He explains that happiness can only be found in God, not the world, which breeds selfishness and violence without God.

In 418 there was an eclipse of the sun followed by earthquakes in Palestine and Languedoc. People again wondered if the end of the world might be close. Again Augustine doubted the end was near, saying that the Lord was not likely to end all just four centuries into the age of Christ.

With all his activities, Augustine was able to found other

monasteries with the rule he had written for his own group in Hippo. That rule was the foundation for more than fifty religious orders in the centuries that followed.

Around 420 civilization was falling apart not only in Africa but in the whole Roman Empire, due to the advance of the various barbarian groups. These barbarians were Arians, who believed that Jesus Christ was more than human but less than divine. This error had been condemned by the Council of Nicea in 325 a.d. In response, Augustine became much stronger in his attacks on the heresies of the day, especially Pelagianism and Arianism.

More Chaos

Augustine had his successor elected in 426, hoping to have more time to write. Alas, the situation in Northern Africa became worse, and his final days were not peaceful. Nonetheless, he spent his final years dictating books night and day with very little sleep. He finished his book, *The City of God* and worked on his book *Revisions*, in which he corrected errors he discovered in all his former writings. He also continued to meditate on the Lord, "day and night" and to write down the thoughts which came to him.

It was during these, his final years, that he accepted the challenge to debate the Arian bishop, Maximinus. The Arian played a devious trick on Augustine. He went on and on in his final arguments, so long that there was not time for Augustine to answer. Then Maximus left, saying he had to get to Carthage, and declared himself victorious. The two agreed to finish the debate by letter, but only Augustine wrote. He wrote a book entitled *Against Maximinus*, which made clear the Arian's errors.

Unfortunately, the Donatists and their violent arm, the Circumcellions, seeing the weakness of the Roman Empire which had condemned them, came forth to renew their terrorism. In addition, the Moors and other groups spread destruction throughout Africa wherever they went. Augustine wrote that Africa, once well-off and well populated, "has fast been turned into a desert."

Because of a conflict with the leaders of Rome, the governor of Africa, Boniface, had made a pact with the barbarians to give them one-third of the Roman land in Africa in return for their help against Rome. This was a huge mistake that Boniface would come to regret. These Vandals, with the violent arm of the Donatists, began to conquer all the coastal towns. Augustine wrote to Boniface appealing to his sense of honor and to his judgement before God for allowing the barbarians to destroy Northern Africa, city by city. Boniface was too proud to change his course and Augustine's plea was ignored, at least for a time.

The people were in great fear of the terrible barbarian sweep of destruction: they begged for Baptism and were seen in public doing penance for their sins. Many fled for their lives. Augustine urged the bishops and priests to stay where they were, and not leave their people without spiritual aid.

Attempts were made to have a truce with the barbarian Vandals, and in fact were successful for a time. However, they were not about to give up their greedy quest for riches which they carried off from every city they ruined. They tore down monasteries, and churches, and burned what remained. They tore apart priests, sisters and monks. They forced mud, lye, vinegar or saltwater down the throats of bishops, and some were burned at the stake. Those who hid in the woods or in the mountains often died there of starvation. Others were seen along the highways naked, begging for food and clothing.

Final Days

By 430 Augustine was on his deathbed, but he kept writing to those who were battling the cruel invasion, encouraging them. The battlers included Boniface, who now was fighting to undo the evil he had invited. In June 430 the barbarians laid siege to Hippo.

As the barbarians advanced, a number of priests and bishops asked Augustine if they should flee to safety. His reply was that although fleeing to safety was an option, their service to their people was of utmost importance and should not be denied. "Therefore," he wrote to his friend, "even if a remnant of the people of God remains in the place [where] we find ourselves, we can only say to the Lord: O God, be our protector and our fortress.'" When Honoratus, Bishop of Thiave asked him for more detail, he said let them all flee together, but if some cannot, let them "endure the [suffering] that the Father of the family wills that they suffer."

At last, the dying bishop was unable to cope with visitors and asked to be alone with his long time friend, Alpyius, who had escaped from Tagaste, now destroyed, where he had been bishop. As Augustine lay dying, he received an invitation from the emperor to represent Africa at the Council of Ephesus. Alas, he was too sick to attend.

He asked for the Penitential Psalms to be copied and tacked on the wall so he could see them and pray them. For his final ten days he asked to be alone, to make his peace with God, and with the exception of the doctor and a brother who came with some little food. On August 28, 430 the churches throughout Hippo were filled with prayers for him. His friends Alypius and Possidius came to sing hymns with him and two other bishops, and as they did so, he died. He was 76 years old. A deep sadness swept the city when his death was made public.

Augustine's feast day is celebrated on the day he died, August 28. His mother's feast is the day before. He is one of the doctors (saints who were great teachers) of the Church. He was constantly writing and his biographer, St. Possidius, listed over 1,000 books, letters and sermons of this great man.

Pope Leo XIII called Augustine the "greatest of the [Church] Fathers." Pope Pius XII said he was "undeniably the greatest Doctor of the Church." And, Pope Paul VI wrote, "The entire thought of Christian antiquity finds a place in his works..." He is the most quoted of all the saints.

Postscript

When Augustine died, the city of Hippo was still under siege by the Vandals, and they seized control of most of Africa in 432. In 439 they conquered all of Africa and sold the Catholic priests as slaves, along with the remaining Roman citizens. In Carthage, they gave the Catholic churches to the Arians. Catholics who refused to become Arian were put to death.

In 455 the Vandal leader Genseric marched triumphantly into Rome. The Vandals and the Moors gathered all the treasures of the city and took them off. Thousands of Romans were captured and brought back to Carthage. In 476 the last Roman emperor, Romulus Augustulus, was deposed by Odoacer, a military leader. By then the empire was so weak that Odoacer felt no need to kill Romulus, but just sent him off to exile.

Although 476 is given as the date for the final fall of Rome, some prefer to date it with the invasion of Alaric in 410, and the destruction of much of the city. It was then that Rome became weak and in great turmoil.

About 250 years after Romulus was deposed the Arabs invaded Northern Africa and destroyed what was left of the Catholic Church there. In 710 Augustine's body was taken away from Hippo to protect it from the Muslim invasion. It eventually ended up in St. Peter's Church in Pavia, Italy.

Reflection

St. Augustine had all the makings of a wild, intellectual playboy. There were two things, however, which saved him from this terrible sort of life. The first was his mother. She could not control him when he became an adult, but she still influenced him. She was able to do that because she herself had shown him the example of what faith could do for a woman who had to overcome the hardship of an unfaithful husband and an obnoxious live-in mother-in-law. He saw in her a strong, unselfish woman who gave her life for the conversion of her husband and his mother.

The second thing in Augustine's favor was his love and search for the truth. Jesus once said, "I am the truth." So it is not surprising that in seeking the truth, no matter what the cost to himself, he was able to find Jesus, who is the source of all truth, and all love. He had to learn the virtue of humility in order to find the truth, a truth he had overlooked for many years in the Catholic Church. And once he learned this wonderful virtue, he found truth, love and peace. Our hearts are indeed restless "until they rest in Him."

Sources

Augustine, St., *The Confessions of St. Augustine*, trans. by John K. Ryan, Garden City, NY: Image Books (Doubleday), 1960, pp. 51-55; 65-68; 80-82; 94; 122-134; 195-203.

Chabannes, Jacques, *St. Augustine*, trans. by Julie Kernan, Garden City, NY: Doubleday, 1962, pp. 42; 135; 136; 145; 160-191; 198-211.

Eberhardt, Newman C., *A Summary of Catholic History: Volume I*, St. Louis, MO: Herder Co., 1961, pp. 186, 213.

Possidius, St., *The Life of St. Augustine Written by The Bishop Possidius*, trans. by Herbert Theberath Weiskotten, from www.tertullian.org/fathers/possidius_life_of_augustine_02_text.htm, pp. 62-65; 96.

Trapè, Agostino, *St. Augustine, Man, Pastor, Mystic*, New York: Catholic Book Publishing Co., 1986, pp. 16, 17; 39, 40; 66-71; 104-160; 183-202; 213-217; 255, 256; 263; 323-333.

Thurston, Herbert J., S. J., and Attwater, Donald, *Butler's Lives of the Saints*, Volume III, Westminster, MD: Christian Classics, 1981, p. 412; 427-431.

Chapter Four

Bl. Miguel Agustin Pro

(1891-1927)

Miguel Pro combined a joyful humor with an intense love for prayer and for serving God's people. In less than two years of ministry in Mexico City, he touched the lives of tens of thousands of people. This was made clear in the throngs who turned out for his funeral procession in defiance of the prohibitions of the Mexican government.

There were eleven children born to Miguel Pro and his wife Josefa Juarez, seven of whom survived infancy. Miguel Agustin was the third child, the oldest of the four boys. Señor Pro was a mine owner, and thus was a wealthy man.

Miguelito, as he was called, loved to visit the mines with his father and go down into the earth for inspections. The boy came to love the mines, and the miners who worked them under harsh conditions. He noticed the harshness and would later be an advocate for the poor miners.

It was in Guadalupe in the state of Zacatecas, Mexico (about 120 miles southwest of Monterrey) that Miguel was born in 1891 and had his first upbringing. When he was just one year old the family moved to Mexico City.

Young Miguel instigated another family crisis some years later when he ate a huge amount of fruit, given him by an Indian woman friend. He became deathly ill, and the doctor told the family the boy would either die, or be terribly handicapped for the rest of his life. For a whole year the boy continued to linger, unable to speak, and hardly knowing his own family members.

When he appeared at the verge of death, his father took the child in his arms and held him before a picture of Our Lady of Guadalupe. He cried out in faith, "My Mother, give me back my son!" The boy was healed.

Miguel was once given a gift of a general's uniform, and when he put it on, took his role quite seriously. He lined up his sisters' dolls and commanded them to move. When they didn't, he stabbed and beheaded them all. Not surprisingly, this did not sit well with his sisters–or his father! He told Miguel, "Well, you will be punished for moving too much!" He received a thrashing for his military feat.

The boy had a particular affection for sweets. He went to the store to buy some, but since he had no money, he charged them to the Pro family account. When the total rose to a sizeable amount, the store owner sent the bill home to the parents. They paid it but young Miguel was again disciplined aptly.

At one point Mrs. Pro said she feared her son would grow up to be another St. Augustine. She hoped he would convert as did Augustine. Miguel assured her he would be another "Agustin" since that was his name.

Miguel did not finish his schooling at this point since his father needed him to help in the office with his mining business. He became most valuable in that capacity, picking up the methods of dealing with time sheets, and all the complexities of mining. He learned to type at the remarkable speed of 100 words per minute. But his favorite respite from the office work was to go down into the mines and be with the miners. He learned to speak their language, and it stayed with him even later in life.

Once, after working all day, he discovered a number of miners were still in the office at 9 pm. Since it was raining outside, he did not want to send them home in the rain, hungry. So, with the permission of his father, he invited the men to stay for dinner. When he told his sisters about his guests, they went into a tizzy since their mother was sick and the servants had gone home. How could they ever prepare a meal for all these men?

Miguel thought fast and came up with a plan. He had his sisters set the table, and he told them he would take care of the food. They were not to enter the kitchen until he was ready. In a short time Miguel entered the dining room with several waiters from the Chinese restaurant carrying a delicious meal. The young boy paid them with his savings and off they went. His sisters were delighted at his ingenuity and generosity.

The Pro family was invited to a mission in a town 15 miles away, and the parents allowed some of the children to go. As they rode off on their donkeys, Miguel took the lead, and warned the sisters not to let the donkey throw them. At one point, however, Miguel's donkey bent down to eat some grass, and young Miguel slid down the donkey's back to a hard landing on the ground. The boy showed his quick thinking to cover his embarrassing mistake by cutting some grass and saying, "I just wanted to get a little grass to give my donkey."

Miguel played the guitar well, and often serenaded his family. He formed a little band with his brothers and sisters and they would play for feast days and anniversaries. He also wrote his own poetry for festive occasions.

The boy loved to go out and watch the musical groups which would march by the house, even when he was in the middle of his studies. His father finally forbade him to leave his books or set foot in the street when he heard the music. So, to enjoy the music without disobeying his father, he would carry his book with him and go on his knees (not his feet!) to watch the musicians go by.

At times the Pro children would be taught at home by a private tutor. One of them was a Protestant woman who was told not to discuss religion. She didn't, but when she was invited to join the family for lunch, Miguel piped up to say the grace out of turn. Then he added a Hail Mary and watched his teacher's silence. At the end, he would add, "What is religion without love of the Blessed Virgin?"

Boarding School Problems

In 1902 a new boarding school was opened in Saltillo and Miguel was sent there. Though it was not a Catholic school, the rector assured Mr. Pro that the boys could practice their religion freely. However, on the first Sunday he was there, Miguel asked to attend Mass. Expressing surprise at such a request, the authorities told the boy that would be impossible. And, every Sunday he was forced to attend the Protestant service.

So, Miguel wrote to his father about the situation. The school authorities intercepted the letter so he never got it. Meanwhile, Miguel refused to attend Protestant services despite the punishment that followed.

When one Sunday Miguel heard a band marching by, he went to the door and while there he saw a family returning from Mass. He called them over and asked them to write to his father and tell him his dilemma. When Mr. Pro got the letter he immediately went to Saltillo, voiced his displeasure in no uncertain terms and removed Miguel from the school.

Upon returning home, the boy exclaimed, "Thus does my Father God deliver me from the greatest difficulties!" This phrase "my Father God" is one he used throughout his life.

Serving The Sick

The holy Mrs. Pro loved to visit the poor sick miner families. She brought her children with her to deliver food and medicine. If they needed a doctor, she paid for one to visit them. In time, she established a free hospital for the poor people. However, once it began to grow the mayor placed so many restrictions on it that the woman had to abandon the project.

Miguel consoled his mother saying, "Never mind, dear momma. When I grow up I'll build you a hospital and we will take care of lots of poor people."

Of course, that dream never came about. However, when Miguel was later a priest, serving in Mexico City, he supported a hundred poor families.

Pranks

Miguel once played a prank on his elder sister Concepción, as they walked along the street. He stopped to knock at the door of a stranger and once they were admitted, he told the owner his sister was fascinated with an (extremely ugly) picture visible through the window.

The owner said it was a family heirloom but for five hundred dollars he would part with it. Miguel said he would take it up with his parents, and escorted his mortified sister to the street. Then he took her for ice cream to make up for his prank.

Another time Miguel and Concepción came upon an auction of stray animals. As they watched, they were auctioning off a lame donkey, missing one ear. One of the onlookers yelled out "One dollar!" and the bidding was on. When it got to two dollars, Miguel yelled "Two and a half dollars!" No one else bid, so Miguel was the winner.

When they led the donkey over to where he had been standing, Concepción was there by herself. Miguel had slipped away. They presented her with the donkey and asked for the $2.50. She tried to explain that she had not made the bid, and that it had been made by her companion but he had disappeared. It took her some time to convince them, but at last she succeeded.

She found her mischievous brother around the corner and he greeted her smiling, "How'd you like the donkey?" He could tell by her face that she was not enjoying the prank. He said, "Forgive me. I admit it was a cruel joke. But, for such pranks we are buddies." Ice cream followed again.

Once when he and his sister Luz were guests at a wedding reception, Miguel spied a table full of sweets. Michael got out of his seat and pretended to be tripped up and fall on the table with the cookies. As he and Luz scrambled to pick them up, he told his sister to pocket a good percentage of the lot. He filled his own pockets as well. Shortly thereafter he invited Luz to go outside with him to take "a little fresh air," not to mention the newly acquired sweets.

When one of his sisters' canaries escaped from its cage she ran to Miguel to have him capture the bird, now perched near the ceiling. Miguel reluctantly agreed, after getting some prodding from his father and as he stretched out to catch the bird in a towel, a whole bunch of cigars fell out of his pockets landing on the head of his father. The whole family burst out laughing to see the boy's smoking habit revealed.

Miguel tried to cover himself by uttering to his father, "Ah, yes... that's a new sample of cigars I brought you to see if you would like them." He handed them over to his father, who responded smiling, "Many thanks."

That evening at dinner, Mr. Pro took out one of the cigars, and said, "Let me try one of the exquisite cigars my son brought me," and proceeded to light it up. Miguel asked to be excused, and once alone with his sister, told her she owed him a box of fancy cigars.

Trapped

Once when Miguel was coming back from a hunting party, he took a shortcut along the railroad tracks. As he hurried along he tripped and got his foot caught in the tracks. He could not break free no matter what he tried, and a train began to approach. He begged Mary Immaculate to save him, promising he would make all sorts of sacrifices to her if she would release him. Finally his boot separated from the sole, and he was free, leaving his sole in the tracks.

Later he said he felt death bearing down on him and saw himself in purgatory. He remarked, "Since then I made an agreement with the Blessed Virgin that she would not let me go to purgatory and I would always be her faithful servant. Ever since she has been my own lady."

A Sweetheart

At age 18 Miguel neglected his religious practices somewhat. His mother, seeing that, arranged for him to deliver a chalice veil which she had sown for the church to the rectory. At first he was reluctant to do so, but he would not go against his mother's wishes.
When he got to the rectory he met three Jesuit priests, one of whom had been a friend of his family. They were on their way to give a mission in a nearby town. They invited him to go with them, so he asked them to come home with him to get permission. Having gotten that, he went off to the mission with a glee which surprised his family.

Shortly after his arrival at the mission the reason for his recent cooling toward religion became clear. His first letter home to his mother was sent by mistake. It was intended for his girlfriend of late, a Protestant girl known to his family. His girlfriend, meanwhile received the letter intended for his mother!

His mother was surprised to get such a casual letter from him. Mrs. Pro realized rather quickly that she had received the wrong letter, and she was unhappy since Miguel had not told her of his new love.

The young woman, who was not particularly religious, was not happy to hear Miguel's rather detailed information on how his heart was touched by God during the mission he was attending, how he felt God's grace descending upon him, how he was planning to make a good confession and receive Holy Communion. She decided to return this letter and all the others he had sent, and end the relationship.

Miguel was far more concerned over the sadness he had brought upon his mother than over the rejection he received from the young woman. His mother returned both letters to the priest at the mission and expressed her disappointment over his secret love. He was so upset about it that he spent the whole night kneeling in prayer before the Blessed Sacrament, asking God's forgiveness.

It seems Miguel had entered this romance on a dare, and once involved, he didn't quite know how to end it. His frustration over his inability to act on his conviction and his hiding all this from his family had caused him to be less jovial and more troublesome with his family.

Of course, he realized it was no great loss that the girl ended it. It had gotten so far that she had promised–lukewarmly–to become a Catholic, but precluded the possibility of warming up to Marian devotion.

At the retreat Miguel really did have an awakening of his faith. He decided to try his hand at being a priest (without bothering with ordination!) so he put on a cassock of one of the priests and went into the town to preach in the houses of the people. It seems he played out his charade well, as the people gave him many gifts for his efforts, including cigars, eggs and cheese. His game ended when the priests saw him one day in his priestly garb as they were going out. They returned him to the retreat house and relieved him of his many donations.

Vocations

Once Miguel was walking with his sister along the road when they saw a truck carrying cauldrons of hot liquefied metal. Miguel led his sister away from the roadway and into a nearby field, giving the truck a wide path, as their father had often instructed them. Once they did so one of the containers tipped over, sending the hot metal down at the very spot where they had been walking. Miguel remarked, "Good thing we were obedient. Otherwise we'd have been burned to death."

Shortly after his life-changing retreat, Miguel and his sisters were staying with relatives when some friends dared the young man to participate in a bullfight. His sisters heard of it and forbade him to do it. He immediately told his friends he couldn't carry out his promise as his sisters had forbade him and he had to follow their orders when away from home. The teasing he got from this was brutal, but Miguel was not swayed.

Once his short-lived romance ended, Miguel had little use for cultivating the affection of other women. And, he had no interest in dancing. When he did attend a dance he would spend much of the time there chatting with his sister in a room apart from the dancing.

In August, 1910 Miguel's sister Luz entered a religious order, the Sisters of the Good Shepherd. It saddened Miguel and his family to lose a family member. Miguel commented, "How wonderful heaven must be to be bought at such a great price." He wept at the absence of his sister from the family table.

Six months later they all attended Luz's reception into the order. Only a few days after that Miguel's closest sister, Concepción decided to enter the same order. The young man wept even more bitterly to lose his "pal" to religious life.

He blamed it all on the Jesuits, who were his sisters' spiritual directors. He declared rashly that he would never forgive them. (Of course, he did.) He went off to live alone in the woods and "lick his wounds." His mother found him in time, and got him to return home.

Once recovered he asked Concepción to take a walk with him. He asked her what moved her to go into the convent. She responded, "The will of God." He answered, "Yes, but that is no answer." He wanted a more earthly answer.

Then he added, "And what about me? What is His will for me?

May I learn it soon. Pray that I may, sister. I must be prepared–that is what God wants."

On the day his sister entered the convent, Miguel's brother received his first Communion. It was February 12, 1911. At the first Communion breakfast Miguel commented, "And why shouldn't I enter the religious life as well? If I have a divine vocation, the matter is settled." After the breakfast, he mentioned his interest in entering religious life to the Mother Superior of his sisters, and asked her to have the sisters pray for his vocation.

It seems that at about this time Miguel entered a Mexican church while a religious Order priest was preaching about the Passion of Christ. "Jesus went through all this for us, and what are we doing for him?" These words went right to the young man's heart. He thought long and hard about what the priest had said. He continued to ask himself, "What have I done for Jesus?" Not long after that he contacted the Jesuits in Santillo.

Miguel went for an interview with a Father Morfin at the Jesuit College. Since the priest was a friend of the family he knew well of Miguel's mischievous antics over the years. So, he decided to test the young man's patience with some antics of his own. When Miguel knocked on his door, he called out, "Come in." However, once his applicant came in he paid no attention to him but continued to read his newspaper. He didn't even invite the young man to sit down.

Miguel stood there seething inside but didn't say a thing. Finally the priest spoke, "Come back tomorrow. I am very busy today" (reading the newspaper?).

The next day Miguel returned and when invited in discovered the priest writing at his desk. Again he said, "Come back tomorrow, young man. I am very busy today." The young man was more angry than before, but he managed to keep his cool. He figured they were just testing his resolve, and he was quite right. So he returned again, and this time Fr. Morfin treated him nicely. After some serious grilling by Morfin and two others, the young applicant was accepted.

Once it was final, Miguel asked the blessing of his parents. They were only too happy to give it. In fact, they were quite aware of his intention for some time and his father went with him to the novitiate to present him to the Order.

On the way to entering the Jesuits, Miguel and his father visited the two sisters at their convent. After embracing his sisters, knowing he would not see them again for a long time, the young man burst into tears and wept a long time. Comforted by his sisters and father, Miguel went on to meet his challenge.

Years later he wrote a poem which seems to summarize the cross he was to bear in leaving his family:

Thy love, 'tis all I claim; it takes the place of gold,
Of glory and of pleasure, fatherland and fame.
To him who feels his warmth all other love is cold,

And with its fire he yearns to set all hearts aflame.

On August 10, 1911 Miguel entered the Jesuit house at El Llano, Michoacan to begin his retreat. His father remained there for the duration of the retreat, and then on August 15, feast of the Assumption, Miguel formally entered the novitiate, and his father set out to return home.

Novitiate

The young novice impressed all around him as being both fun-loving and prayerful. One classmate described him as of "good humor" and in possession of a "witty eloquence." He continued to be a great mimic, and used his talent to entertain his fellow novices. He wore two hats, so to speak: one that of the joyful humorist and singer, the other that of a "Carthusian monk," spending more time than any of the others in the chapel.

One day his friend suggested they spend more time at recreation since they were permitted, as they had eaten late. Miguel declined, saying, "No, because I would lose my vocation. If I don't take a siesta I'll be sleepy at prayer, and if I don't pray, I'll lose my vocation." How very true!

Novice masters often can be harsh with their novices, and it was no different with Miguel's, Fr. Manuel Santiago. He would often rebuke the young novice for the slightest mistakes or flaws, but Miguel took it all well. He commented, "When I entered the Society I sacrificed my reputation to God."

Once Fr. Santiago strongly reprimanded the young novice. Shortly thereafter Brother Miguel went to the priest's room, knocked on his door, and when invited in he begged forgiveness for his fault.

Another day at recreation Brother Pro climbed a pole and began to preach to his classmates as they were playing ball. They all stopped and came over to hear his cleverly conceived message. When Fr. Santiago walked by he asked why the commotion, and was told what was happening. He commented, "What a pity that I arrived when the sermon was over. I hope Brother Pro will repeat it for me." He did, quite embarrassed.

After two years of novitiate, Miguel made his vows with his classmates on the feast of the Assumption, August 15, 1913. Right after that, Mexico began to undergo great upheaval and persecution of the Church began in earnest.

Granada and Nicaragua

Just one year after the young men made their vows they had to leave El Llano because of the danger to the community posed by the revolutionaries. Miguel and three companions traveled to Guadalajara where they were reunited with fourteen of their brother novices from

El Llano. Happily, Miguel was able to spend time with his mother, who was also in Guadalajara in exile with four of her children. Made destitute, she was working as a laborer, something she had never had to do before. But, she made no complaint.

Miguel did all in his power to bring some cheer to his family and his Jesuit brothers. However, his stay there would not last. On October 2 the brothers left Guadalajara for the United States. Miguel expressed a warm farewell to his mother and siblings. He would never see his mother again.

The young novices were welcomed at Los Gatos, California, where they continued their studies. Even there Miguel showed an irrepressible zeal for souls. On one of their customary walks around the city, they met a group of gypsies. He pulled out his guitar and began to play for them. Then he told some stories following which he taught them about God and how much he loved them. Finally, he gave each of the children some candy.

In June, 1915, the novices were directed to leave for Spain. They got to Granada in late July. They would spend five years there, studying rhetoric for two years and philosophy for three more.

The fact that he was not yet a priest did not hold him back from performing works of mercy for the people in and around Granada. On his vacations he would get permission from his superiors to visit the sick and bring them food. During one such period he would visit a poor, sick man and bring him eggs and fruit. He spoke eloquently of

God and prepared the man to receive the sacraments.

He would also visit the home for the aged run by the Little Sisters of the Poor. He would do the humble tasks of washing their clothes, sweeping floors, and making beds. And, of course, he would teach the residents the catechism.

He took every opportunity as well to teach the young about God. He was full of fun, so the children loved to listen to him, and he was an expert at making religion understandable to all. All of this flowed from his almost constant prayer, especially on his knees before the Blessed Sacrament.

During an epidemic of the "Spanish Flu" Miguel volunteered to be infirmarian so he could care for the sixty-plus scholastics (seminarians) who were stricken. He cared for his sick brothers night and day, cheering them up, entertaining them at every opportunity. Since he was caring for the sick he himself was quarantined for the two weeks he served them. In the end, he also caught the disease.

Once he finished his study of philosophy, he was sent to Nicaragua, to serve in a college. A number of things worked against him there, including the weather, the poor behavior of the students, the poisonous snakes, and his own health problems. The many scorpions falling from the ceiling in the dormitories, and the leaky roofs during rainstorms caused them all many sleepless nights as well.

Here he was also falsely accused of serious misbehavior, and had to go through the grueling process of defending himself. In the end he was cleared, but the trial took its toll.

Theology and Ordination

After two years Miguel returned to Barcelona, Spain, to study theology. Again here, his jovial and friendly ways won him many friends among his classmates. It was during this period, which lasted two years, that Miguel and three classmates were given permission to make the "spiritual exercises" made famous by St. Ignatius himself. They made them at Manresa, where Ignatius had written them. They prayed for hours at a stretch and one of the brothers commented later on how Miguel did great penances during this retreat.

The final year of his preparation for the priesthood was spent in Enghein, Belgium. It is said that during this time he deepened his commitment to the life of prayer, and began to spend even more time before the Blessed Sacrament.

Miguel also performed a small act of charity each day for his classmates during their vacation. He would walk each day the three miles to the post office in Enghien to mail their letters and pick up their mail. It was often raining when he went but he joked about his effort in the rain.

At Enghein he went through great spiritual trials of dryness. He also feared that his ordination would be delayed. His health problems grew worse during this time as well.

All was forgotten when he was "called to Sacred Orders" in the early summer of 1925. He was ordained a priest on August 31, 1925. Despite the fact that he could not give his first priestly blessing to his family members who were so far away, he was filled with joy to finally be a priest of God. He was 34 years old.

He offered his first Mass the next day, September 1 with great devotion. His love for the Mass was indicated in a letter he wrote to a friend about to be ordained. He wrote, "I have not found in all my religious life a more rapid or effective means of living very closely united with Jesus than the holy Mass." This affection was even more evident in a letter he wrote to another young man preparing for priesthood:

For about a year now I have had the happiness of saying Mass; the joy that one feels is like nothing in this world below; it is something higher, something spiritual and divine... There is something in me which I had never felt before, and which makes me see things in another manner; this is not the fruit of studies or of our holiness, more or less solid, nor of anything that has a personal or human seal. It comes from the priestly character which the Holy Spirit impresses in our souls; it is a closer participation in the divine life which raises and deifies us; it is a higher force which makes available the desires and aspirations which we had been unable to realize before.[2]

When he became quite sick later on Miguel got permission to say Mass every day, and volunteered to say the earliest Mass. He said, "I can't sleep anyway so it is not much of a sacrifice for me to get up early." He would often spend whole nights in prayer, waiting for sleep. After a quick breakfast he would return to the chapel to assist at other Masses.

Although he was limited in what he could do to save souls because he was not yet fluent in French, he did what he could. He wrote to a friend, "On the day of my ordination I asked but one thing of God–to be useful to souls."

The Communists

Once he found himself on a train in a car filled with socialists. He entered and began to talk with them.

One of them commented, "But monseigneur l'Abbé, we are all socialists!"

He answered, "I will be happy to travel with you since I too am a socialist." The men were taken aback. "Yes, gentlemen, I'm a socialist, but not like you, who do not know what the word means.

---

[2]Adapted from M. D. Forrest, MSC, *The Life of Father Pro*, Lexington, KY: St Pius X Press, 1944, pp. 53, 54.

Can any of you tell me exactly what a socialist is?"

One of the answers was that a socialist was one who wanted to take money from the rich. "Then you are robbers?" asked Miguel with a twinkle in his eye. "If so, tell me, so I can get off this train."

This brought a laugh from the men. One of them asked the priest if he were not afraid of them.

"Afraid of you?" he asked. "Don't you know I carry a better weapon than a revolver?"

"Show it to us, priest-socialist."

He pulled out a crucifix and held it up, saying, "You should know that all of you together can do nothing to me unless the Lord wants or allows it. With him on my side I fear nothing. And I'm sure that I cause you more fear than you do me."

Their smiles vanished and one said, "And what do you think of the communists?"

The young priest replied, "I think that they, like the socialists, are deluded."

"But we are also communists."

"So much the better for me, as it's now one o'clock and I have nothing to eat. Since I am also a communist, I am going to have a banquet with the meal you're carrying."

Realizing that he had called them to practice what they preached, they laughed. Having arrived at their stop, they wished Miguel well, shook his hand and got off the train. Before the train moved again, one got back on to give the young priest a bag of chocolates. He had won their affection, if not their political sway.

Early Ministry

Three months after his ordination, Miguel's health condition got much worse. He had been quietly enduring a stomach ailment for some years prior to ordination, but now it became clear he needed a serious operation to prevent further deterioration. Knowing the operation would put him in danger of death, he commented to a friend, "I am prepared to die now."

The operation was unsuccessful, so another was carried out, this time without anesthesia. Despite the excruciating pain, the young priest made no outward sign of his suffering with the exception of two tears which rolled down his cheeks. He held a crucifix tightly in his hand. A third equally painful operation was necessary, and was carried out in January, 1925. Again, he was stoic in his agony.

On February 8, just a short time after his third painful operation, he received the heart-rending news that his mother had died. He had received a letter from her only weeks earlier, stating that her health was failing and she would probably never get to see him at the altar. He stayed composed when he received the news, but later on in private, holding his crucifix tightly he poured out tears of grief over her death. His grieving would continue for some time as he suffered, in his words, "a void that nothing in this world will be able to fulfill."

At one point he was able to visit a young man who was staunchly anti-clerical. He hated priests because he had been unjustly expelled from his school by a priest. Fr. Pro showed him nothing but kindness and in time got him to tell his story. He gained his trust so that he could teach the young man the faith and after a month he received his first Communion.

Miguel was permitted to visit Lourdes before returning to Mexico. He described his Lourdes experience as follows: "This has been one of the happiest days in my life... I spent an hour in the Grotto... I wept like a baby." A few days later, on June 24, 1926 the young priest boarded a ship to return to his native Mexico, where terrible persecution of the Church was spreading throughout the whole country.

Return to Mexico

Plutarco Calles had become president of Mexico in 1924. He quickly began to enforce the "Constitution of Queretaro" an anti-Catholic set of laws that had not been enforced very strongly. He added his own extreme laws against religion in 1926. These would include secularizing all education, dissolving all religious Orders, forbidding priests to criticize the government or the laws of the country even in private meetings, declaring seminary studies of no academic standing, restricting public worship to within churches (this is known today as "freedom of worship") and under government supervision, and declaring all churches, monasteries, convents and other church buildings to belong to the government.

Because of this decree, the Church went underground. That is, public worship in the churches was suspended, to protect the priests from persecution, but worship and the sacraments would continue in homes and various other secret sites.

Father Miguel Pro arrived in his native Mexico July 7, 1926. Strangely, the priest was permitted to enter without his passport or his luggage being scrutinized. Miguel wrote of his surprise:

By an extraordinary permission of God I was able to re-enter my native country. The government being what it is, expelling priests and religious, I don't know how I managed to get in. The Board of Health passed me over. No one examined my passports. The customs officer did not even glance at my baggage.[3]

The young priest first reported to his Provincial and received his

[3]M. D. Forrest, MSC, *The Life of Father Pro*, p. 65; Antonio Dragon, S. J., *Miguel Agustin Pro of The Society of Jesus*, English trans. by Lawrence Drummond, Montreal: The Messenger Press, 1930, p. 89.

assignment in Mexico. Then he went to visit his family, his father, his brother Roberto and his sister, Ana Maria.

Then he went to pursue his ministry to God's people. This, despite his being quite sick still from his trip across the ocean, and his three operations. The churches would be closing in just three weeks, so he began to spend long hours in the confessional: 5:30 am to 11 am and 3:00 pm to 8 pm. Twice during this time he fainted out of weakness and he had to be carried out of his confessional. Once recovered, he went right back in for more.

He wrote in a letter about all this: "My confession was a jubilee. Twice they took me out because I fainted, for my animal nature which had just left the enticing cushions of a hospital, was not accustomed to the hard seat of the confessional. And, besides, the heat and stuffiness were oppressive."

Also during these three weeks he taught, preached and counseled those who came to him. This period was one of ceaseless activity for the people. When the 31st of July arrived, he offered the holy Mass for the final time in a church. From then on he would have to serve God's people in secret.

Underground Ministry

The young priest established "Communion Stations" all across Mexico City where good Catholics lived, and would host a Mass in their home when Miguel would come. They also were privileged to have the Blessed Sacrament reserved there. All this was done at great peril to the host family, with all in attendance being discovered and severely punished. Of course, the greatest danger was for the priest himself.

Father Pro would give Communion to two or three hundred people each day. On First Fridays that number would swell to anywhere between 700 and 1200 persons.

He performed Baptisms, officiated at weddings (one of a couple who had lived together for 25 years), heard confessions, visited the sick. He preached sermons and gave retreats as well, risking death at every turn.

He trained three hundred laymen to go about the city and beyond to give talks on the faith. Humbert, the brother of Fr. Pro was a member of this group, who risked their lives to promote the faith.

Because all the Catholic schools had been closed, several hundred catechists were prepared by the priests and others to travel across Mexico teaching the children. They reached about 11,000 young children. One priest was shot when the police discovered a photo of him giving first Communion to a little one. Before he was executed he cried out, "Onward! Suffering lasts but a moment; glory is eternal."

A classmate spoke of Fr. Pro's herculean efforts during the sixteen months he was able to serve, saying he did the work of seven priests.

At one point when the persecution was raging, Miguel wrote in a letter, "The Mexican Goliath will soon lose his head by means of the shepherd's staff which the unarmed people of Guadalupe carry, and then Christ alone will reign, Christ alone will conquer, Christ alone will command... from all sides comes news of outrages and reprisals... the number of martyrs is increasing day by day... Oh! If that could be my lot!"

In another letter he wrote, "What a blessing if I could join those who are to be hanged at Pagasos del Zocalo; that would settle my final examination." (He did not get to take his final examination at Enghein since his superior had directed him to return to Mexico before he could take it.)

When Fr. Pro was told he would be sent to the US for his "second novitiate" he wrote to his provincial:

In a previous letter you indicated I would leave here by June or July. Don Carlos (a pseudonym for his immediate Jesuit superior, used to protect his identity) has said nothing to me of this. Would it be too much curiosity for me to ask your intention? You know I have no preference for anything in particular, and although it would be a grief to lose the opportunity I have here of going to heaven... I much prefer to obey, because thus I shall achieve much more for those I want to serve.

Without wanting to influence your decision, and always under obedience, I will say what Crivelli said in Rome: "Permit me to stay at my post until this persecution passes."

Fr. Pro's request was granted. He stayed in Mexico City.

Helping The Poor and Avoiding Capture

In retaliation against the Calles oppression of the Church and all people of faith, the Mexicans called for a boycott of goods and services. They cut their spending to the bone, and gave up shows, movies, bullfights, races, unnecessary driving, and expensive food and clothing. They withdrew all their money from the banks. Within one month 27 million pesos were withdrawn from banks and moved to foreign banks. Factories whose owners were anti-religious lost all their customers.

The Minister of Finance resigned. There were leaflets and stickers all over urging everyone to join the boycott. Calles shut down printing companies suspected of producing the leaflets and stickers, and jailed the owners. So, the youth printed them in basements by night. Some were copied on typewriters. A secret radio station was begun for broadcasting Catholic programs.

One old merchant displayed a poster in his window reading, "Christ lives! Christ reigns! Christ commands!" When told by soldiers to remove it, he refused. He was shot to death on the spot.

Miguel often had a bunch of pro-religion leaflets in his pockets. Once he was arrested while his pockets were stuffed with them. On the way to the police station, the priest engaged the driver in a lively conversation and every so often he threw out the window some of the leaflets. All were gone by the time they arrived. Another time he pinned a leaflet on his back and slowly walked through a streetcar so all could see the leaflet. Everyone assumed that he was unaware that the leaflet had been pinned to his coat.

Those handing out leaflets were subject to being shot on the spot. The execution of two young boys jolted the nation. A secret Calles supporter asked of them their religious views. When they answered he had them arrested and shot.

The people were not intimidated by such savagery. Fifty thousand participated in a pilgrimage to Our Lady of Guadalupe. Over two hundred thousand gathered to celebrate the feast of Christ the King.

Twice Miguel was captured and put in jail. Neither time did they suspect he was a priest since he always dressed as a layman. The first time he was set free when he showed the jailers the scars on his stomach from his surgeries. They felt sorry for him.

The second time was following the release of 600 balloons with religious leaflets attached. It seems the police suspected that they had originated from the house where Miguel was staying. They decided to arrest anyone who entered there that day. So, when he got there they took him in. He gave his correct name, Miguel Agustin Pro.

The jailer proclaimed, "Tomorrow we will have Mass."

"Bad, very bad," thought Miguel. "They've already recognized me!"

"Mass?" they all inquired. "Yes," said the jailer, "as one of you is a priest."

"Bad, *very* bad," thought Miguel, as the prisoners looked at each other wondering.

"His name is Miguel Agustin."

Miguel replied, "Stop! I am Miguel Agustin, but there is as much chance of my saying Mass tomorrow as my sleeping on a mattress tonight."

"Well what about your putting 'presbitero' after your name?"

"Pro is simply my last name," answered the priest. "Pbro is the abbreviation for presbitero." That ended that.

That night, they all slept on the hard cement of the (outdoor) prison yard. They huddled together beneath the stars as it was a cold night. They sang some hymns and prayed the rosary before falling asleep. The jailers threw pails of water on them in the morning to awaken them. It was no easy night, or morning either.

They cross-examined the young priest twice but he evaded their questions and even injected a bit of humor into the process, so they could find no reason to keep him. When the jailers asked him if he were prepared to pay a large fine, his answer was bold. "No, for two reasons. First I haven't a cent. And, second, even if I had, I would not like to have lifelong remorse for having contributed... to keep in power the present government for even ten millionth of a second." The young priest wondered later why he was not shot for saying that. Nonetheless, he was released about noon.

It was not easy for the authorities to find the elusive priest. He had four different places where he would spend his nights. He received mail and messages at each of them, as well as "beans for destitute families."

At one point he organized six women and six men to raise money and provide for the poor. He himself raised money to pay the rent of as many as 96 families. He would carry gifts of food himself to those in need: he once carried six hens and a turkey to them! He took in abandoned babies and found them homes. He brought food and blankets to prisoners and found doctors to provide free services to the needy.

The first abandoned baby he placed with a family was a great challenge, as he described:

I had no time to send anyone for the baby, and I had to take it myself. I was so imprudent as to put it, well wrapped in a large scarf, in a corner of the car. At the first bump, the baby bounced up and had I not caught it on the fly, I would have had to bring it to the morgue. I took it in my arms and I need not tell you what a state I was in when I handed it to its adoptive parents![4]

He wrote in a letter,

...without knowing how, or when or who the benefactor is, I receive at one time fifty kilos of sugar, at another, boxes of biscuits, or coffee, chocolate, rice, and even wine... And the providence of God is so fatherly that while I am searching my head, wondering whom I can go to in order to 'sting' him for a donation, I find the storeroom filled. The best thing is that [I] don't appear out in front: I pull the strings and other generous souls do everything."[5]

"One day," he wrote elsewhere, "I was walking with a handbag of a lady that was very pretty (the handbag, not the lady). It had been given me five minutes before. Then I met a much painted lady who asked me what I was carrying. I replied that it was a lady's handbag, worth twenty-five pesos, but I would let her have it for fifty pesos. I asked her to send the money to a certain poor family. She agreed on the spot."

---

[4]Antonio Dragon, S. J., *Miguel Agustin Pro of The Society of Jesus*, p. 117.

[5]M. D. Forrest, MSC, *The Life of Father Pro*, p. 85.

In another letter he remarked, "From four to six is the smallest number in a family, and from ten to twelve the greatest. They have a bad habit of eating three times a day, and generally with good appetites. They live in houses for which rent must be paid. They use shoes which wear out and they wear clothes which take on holes; and they know how to get sick and ask for medicine.

Clearly there is not... enough money for all these needs; but I impose on doctors who are my friends, and on rich people who lend me houses for six or eight months with stamped receipts for rent. Alas, I have no friends among shoemakers or tailors, so I must calculate six pairs of shoes at twelve pesos cost seventy-two pesos. And I have only twenty pesos.[6]

It was difficult for Miguel to go around begging, given his family background–namely upper class. Nonetheless, he did lots of begging, and with great effect.

Hiding Out

After just six months of his whirlwind efforts for the faith, the authorities issued an order for his arrest. He was made "public enemy

---

[6]Forrest, p. 86.

number one" for his extraordinary effectiveness. As a result, his superior ordered him to keep out of sight for a while. He obeyed, but was not happy about it.

So, he wrote to the provincial, his superior's superior. He wrote as follows:

Shut up in a small room with no wider horizon than a neighboring corral, prohibited from going around, I pass the days reading my books and papers and studying.

Obedience is better than sacrifices and therefore I have not moved from where I am; nevertheless, permit me to say one thing, without appearing in any way to criticize or murmur. The situation here is very delicate; there are dangers for all and I know that God wishes us to help ourselves that he may help us. Still, the people are in great need of assistance... To contribute with my grain of sand would be known publicly if I acted as before; but with discretion and moderation it does not appear to me a rash undertaking... I think there is a medium between rashness and fear, and also between extreme prudence and audacity...

I know that I am doing more for the persecuted Church by staying in my room out of obedience than by going into the middle of the public square by my own will; but it is not disobedience to ask of my Provincial permission to do something, and to ask it in spite of the order of my immediate superior. Judge for yourself, Father, and rest assured that I shall in all things carry out your orders and those of Don Carlos [his immediate superior].[7]

Freed to Serve Again

His letter won the day. He wrote to his friend,

With intense delight I received permission to leave the hiding place I had been forced to take up by the Illustrious Mr. Calles of Plutarchs (the anti-Catholic president).

I was constantly hearing the complaints of those around me, who lamented the imprisonment of this person, the exile of that one, and the murder of yet another... and there I was caged... and burning to throw myself into the battle and give new life to the great champions of our faith, with the hope that, perhaps, their misfortune might be my lot also. But that honey was not

---

[7]Forrest, pp. 88, 89.

brought to the lips of the donkey [i.e., Miguel himself], and I had to resign myself and offer my desires to God on the altar of obedience."[8]

So, once set free from his "cage" the young priest went on a tear giving retreats. He described this in a letter:

I got revenge on my forced isolation by giving retreats right and left, a most beautiful ministry, but rather frightening to me because I had never exercised it. I began humbly, as a kind of experiment, with 78 pious old women, who with their ejaculations and sighs, their sobs and groans, made me realize that if I controlled the chords of feelings in others, I also managed to suppress the laughter in my own humanity. The laughter was so bubbling up within me on seeing the tearful faces and spasms of woe, that I judged it wiser to cut loose from the feminine gender to go over to the masculine.[9]

And indeed, I got too much of the masculine–some fifty noisy chauffeurs, the kind with the Texan hats and the shaggy hair who do a lot of spitting–fine types with their rough, unpolished

---

[8]Forrest, p. 89.

[9]Forrest, p. 90.

manners... To my great surprise, I found that in talking to these chaps, the language and slang of the common people flowed easily from my lips–I thought that after so many years I had forgotten it, as I had left the mines sixteen years before...[10]

Pardon my dwelling on the solemnity of these lectures: in a large yard with the usual junk lying around, myself clothed as a mechanic with a cap pulled down to my eyebrows, and giving a spiritual shove to my responsive audience. God bless the taxi drivers of all the world![11]

Later he gave a retreat for about 80 "teachers and other government employees." He wrote to his friend,

I would like to see you here, pestered by a similar pack of hounds, who denied the existence of hell, and the immortality of the soul, who gloried in a rabid self-sufficiency and refused to submit to the sweet truths of our religion. I sweat ink [Spanish idiom for struggling hard], I admit, but I was more than repaid by seeing them all receive the sacraments...

---

[10]Forrest, p. 91; Dragon p. 121.

[11]Forrest, pp. 90, 91.

I could feel the grace of God alone working; all the force of my arguments, all my efforts, my thrusts, my explosions to make an impression were useless. I saw that the grace of God touched these souls through simple phrases which I coined at the moment... I counted more than a dozen very remarkable conversions... Blessed be my Father God who is so wonderfully good![12]

Fr. Miguel continued to hear confessions all over, including that of a tramp in a public park. Once he wrote to his superior:

It is 3 O'clock. I should be in the confessional–a rather hard task nowadays. The Heavenly Father has given me a severe penance in the form of a toothache–so violent at times that I feel like hurling the confessional screen at the poor penitent... but I must pay interest on all the favors granted to my large family![13]

The "interest," of course was the penance he had to offer for the souls he was saving. His large family? All those he was serving.

He offered more Masses in peoples' homes, officiated at weddings,

---

[12]Forrest, p. 91.

[13]Dragon, p. 129.

baptized babies, and preached in addition to the retreats. He was often bringing the sacraments and material aid to the sick or dying as well as before.

He often got into the jails disguised to visit those arrested for their faith. He would bring them food, blankets and wine, in addition to absolution for their sins in confession. This "criminal," wanted by the police, was ministering to his people right under the nose of the authorities. He wrote, "If the jailers only knew what sort of bird I am!"

The young priest always dressed as a layman. Had he dressed as a priest, he would have been arrested on the spot. He traveled around on a bicycle, off of which he fell from time to time, causing minor injuries.

Close Calls

Once Padre Miguel was giving Communion at 6:30 am at a private home, when someone shouted "Police!" Before the people could panic, the priest told everyone to keep calm and to go into various rooms in the house and remain quiet. He put a cigar in his mouth and went to meet the police.

"There is a public service here!" claimed a policeman.

"Don't broadcast it." answered the priest, dressed in a gray suit.

They repeated, "There is a public service here."

Miguel remarked, "Look, my friends, they have sent you on a wild goose chase."

"But I saw a priest come in here."

"Ah, how you love to talk. Will you bet a beer there's a priest here?" answered the priest, unfazed.

"We have an order to search the house. Come along with us," demanded the policeman.

"So that's all I have to do, follow you? And on whose order? Show me the name. Go on yourselves through the house, and when you find that fellow, 'Public Service' come and tell me so that I might attend Mass," said the priest with a mischievous boldness.

Nonetheless, he followed the police through the house, as they thought he was the owner. His charade almost cost him, as he was unfamiliar with the house and he twice identified rooms incorrectly before entering: one drawing room he stated was a bedroom, and one bathroom he said was a sewing room!

Needless to say they found no priest, or no *other* priest. The Padre said he would have been happy to work with them until they found the audacious priest, had he not a woman he had to meet shortly. The police posted a guard at the door of the house, while Fr. Pro went to give Communion to other people. When he returned, the police had not yet nabbed the priest they were seeking.

Another time he saw two policemen outside a house he was approaching in which he was to say Mass. His first thought was "My time is up!" But, so as not to abandon his friends who awaited him, he decided to try something. He walked up to the house, wrote down the house address, and opened his vest pretending to show a secret service badge and said, "There is a cat bagged here." The police saluted him and let him in the house.

Those in the house were afraid when they saw him, knowing the police were outside the door, but he reassured them. "We couldn't be safer. The police themselves are guarding the house." He was willing to say Mass, but the people begged him to escape through the roof. He would have none of their escape plan: he walked calmly past the police and received a salute as he walked by.

Once after giving a retreat to government employees, he was leaving about 9:30 pm and he noticed two detectives cross the street and wait for him at the corner. He went up to them and asked for a light for his cigarette. Unwilling to help the object of their pursuit, they replied, "You can get a match in the store."

As he walked off, he noticed they followed him at every turn. He hailed a taxi, and so did they. His driver was Catholic and so was willing to help him shake his pursuers. So he instructed the driver, "Slow down at the corner I point out. I'll jump out and you proceed on."[14]

The fugitive took off his hat and unbuttoned his coat so that his

---

[14]Forrest, pp. 96.

white shirt showed, thereby changing his appearance. He jumped out and leaned on a tree, making sure he could be seen. "The detectives passed by a second later, almost grazing me with the mudguards of their car; they saw me, but it never dawned on them who I was." He turned and went on his way.[15]

Once two detectives tasked with capturing the elusive priest approached him. They figured they had their man until he greeted them so courteously and casually that they began to wonder. He invited them to lunch and once there, he offered a toast to their good health.

Another time the priest noticed two policemen running after him. When he turned the corner, he saw a woman he knew walking along, and with a wink and a "Let's pretend," began to walk arm in arm with her down the street. When the police came around the corner, they stopped in their tracks. It appeared that the object of their chase was just going to meet his sweetheart! Once they had gone off, Miguel explained the situation to his friend, and went off to continue his ministry.

A certain difficult woman he had to deal with seemed like an impossible challenge:

Once I had to listen for an hour to the erratic words of a woman

---

[15]Forrest, p. 96, 97.

who was a religious philosopher. She poured forth the wildest abusive words that human lips could utter. I had never heard anything so fierce, even among the miners. And yet she was quite ill. She blasphemed and cursed everything sacred: the saints, the sacraments, even the Virgin Mary's most blessed name. I strove to convert her truly demonic tongue. At the end of six days she recited nothing but Hail Mary's and the Creed... Very likely she will die tomorrow as a result of an operation, but I will bring her Holy Communion early.

He wrote that at one point he tangled with an army reservist who swore by the fifteen peers of France (nobility) that he (Miguel) would go to jail. Miguel responded, "Listen, you bore, if you bring me to jail I will be unable to hear your mother's confession."

"Pardon, Father. You see what time we are living in. Quit this place as quickly as possible!"

"Quit? You quit, and without even completing your search. Go and tell your mother I'll be at her house tonight to hear her confession, and tomorrow I'll bring her Communion. Let us hope we will soon hear *your* confession..."

Miguel wrote further, "The following day my friend was at his mother's Communion. I hope to bring him the same blessing..."

He guided many souls who were enduring great crosses. He always treated them with gentle care. Once when he came home late and was exhausted, he remembered he had not prayed the Breviary. He thought of one of his suffering penitents and he fell on his knees and prayed it, offering his tired effort for her.

Prepared for Martyrdom

Just two months before his martyrdom, Father Pro went to say Mass for some nuns. He asked them to pray that God would allow him to offer his life for Calles, for priests and for Mexico. The Mass, he said, would be offered for that intention. One of the sisters wrote later, "During the entire Mass he was filled with emotion. He shed tears the whole time. At the end of the Mass he told one of the nuns, 'I don't know if it's my imagination or if it actually occurred, but I feel clearly that the Lord has accepted my offer.'"

He wrote a prayer to the Blessed Virgin asking his martyrdom of her. What follows is an abbreviated version of it.

My Mother... In my life I wish for the scoffing and mockery of Calvary; I wish the slow agony of your Son; the contempt, the ignominy the infamy of the cross; I long to stand at your side, virgin most sorrowful, strengthening my spirit with your tears, consummating my sacrifice with your martyrdom, sustaining my heart with your sorrow, loving your God and my God with the immolation of my being. Amen.

Calles

Before speaking of the final period of Fr. Miguel's life, we digress for a few moments to explain the man Plutarco Calles, the self-proclaimed enemy of Fr. Pro and the Catholic Church. He was born on Christmas in 1877. He became a teacher in public school and became the treasurer of the Teacher's Association. When all the money vanished he was fired.

Not long afterward a relative arranged for Plutarco to be treasurer of the town of Guaymas. He was again fired for stealing and was almost jailed for his crime.

His next job was as a bartender at the local hotel. He was rather quickly promoted to manager of the hotel. Shortly thereafter the hotel burned to the ground. He was charged with arson, but somehow he again evaded punishment, even though the insurance company refused to make full payment.

He next became manager of his uncle's ranch, and then a flour mill. Both went bankrupt shortly after he took over. It seems that handling money was not his strong point!

By 1912 Plutarco had entered politics. Latching on to the revolution of Francisco Madero, he became chief of police in a small town on the Mexican border with Arizona. His viciousness was firmly established when he arrested a poor, insignificant peasant for shouting "Down with Madero." Calles had him hanged by barbed wire from a railroad bridge. His cruelty was even more firmly established when he had Manuel Huerta, who had pardoned him from his embezzling crime, captured by his agents from American soil, and returned to Mexico where he was hanged.

In 1913 he joined with the revolution led by Alvaro Obregón and soon was chosen to be commander of the Sonora army. In 1915 he was made governor of Sonora by revolutionary Carranza. In 1919 he was named secretary of Industry, Commerce and Labor. Soon after, he resigned this post and in 1920 he aligned himself with the presidency of General Obregón.

Calles then played a part in the ruthless murder of Carranza. This made it possible for Obregón to declare himself president of Mexico in 1920. Thus began what was known as the "Rule by Cynicism" as Obregón tipped his hat somewhat to the revolution by taking over large landholdings of the rich, and paid off his supporters. He was smart enough to win the favor of American business concerns by accommodating their call for just treatment of their Mexican business enterprises.

However, Obregón was not bold enough to try to go against the constitution and seek another consecutive term. So, he put up his friend Plutarco Calles for the office, and having killed his opponents by poisoning or other means, Calles took over. Their military successes were assured by the weapons provided by the US on credit as a reward for protecting their interests.

So Calles took office in 1924. His platform: "dictatorship of the proletariat; suppression of private property; total submission of the family to the state; the uprooting of all religion."

Under Calles, thousands who could afford to do so left Mexico. Those who stayed to oppose the vicious dictator were hunted down and once found were subject to brutal torture and murder. No one who opposed the horrific Calles regime was safe.

Mexico had about 3,000 priests before the rebellion began. By 1934 there were just 344. Forty priests were executed and many others exiled. All decent people were under a great and oppressive cloud beginning with the rule of Pularco Calles and beyond.

The Attempted Assassination

The event that set in motion the wheels leading to Miguel Pro's martyrdom took place November 13, 1927. On that Sunday afternoon, at 2 pm General Alvaro Obregón, former "president" of Mexico and presidential candidate for the next election was on his way to a bullfight with some friends. From a car passing by a bomb was thrown into the general's car and shots were fired at him. The men in the general's car fired back. Surprisingly, Obregón was not hurt.

Four men were in the attacking car. Nahum Ruiz received a bullet in his head and remained unconscious until he died seven days later. Antonio Tirado was caught and put to death on November 23. When

Luis Segura Vilchis heard that the Pro brothers had been captured and were suspected of being part of the plot, he surrendered to the police and admitted he was the master-mind of the attempt. He declared that the Pro brothers had nothing to do with their effort. He was executed November 23. The fourth person in the car, the driver, was never captured.

The government officials had been unable up to this point, to discover where Miguel was living. He had eluded the police by moving from one residence to another, staying only a few days at each before moving on.

On November 17 Mrs. J. Montes de Oca was arrested in connection with her renting a house in which bomb making materials were found. She was put in jail for questioning. In the interrogation that ensued, every effort was made to clear Mrs. Montes. (She was banished from Mexico after Fr. Pro's death.)

In the process, it seems that they brought in Mrs. Montes' son, José for questioning. He revealed that the woman the police had seen with his mother was Ana Maria Pro, sister of Miguel. Also, after being beaten by the police, and with the threat of his mother being jailed, the young man told them where the Pro brothers were staying at the time. In the spring Calles had called for the capture of Fr. Pro, whatever the cost. Calles officials were delighted to get the information, and decided to arrest them right away.

Meanwhile, Miguel had arranged for his brothers to depart to the

United States on November 18. He planned to resume his ministry on the 19th. However, this was not to be.

Arrest

On November 18, at 4 am a police officer and some soldiers burst into the house where Fr. Miguel and his two brothers, Humberto and Roberto, were sleeping and arrested all three. "Who are you?" asked Fr. Pro.

"Alvaro Basail, agent of the General Inspection of Police," answered the leader. "Are you the Pro brothers?"

"Yes," they responded.

All their guns were drawn and pointed at the brothers. Basail said, "I arrest you."

Humberto, fearful they might shoot him on the spot, said, "I want to go to confession."

"Not allowed," replied the officer.

"Allowed or not, I'll hear him," responded the priest quietly.

Miguel moved to a corner of the room and heard Humberto's confession, then that of Roberto.

The three were then hauled off to jail. Miguel and Roberto were put in one cell with some other Catholics. Humberto was in another multi-prisoner cell.

Obregón doubted that the Pro brothers had been involved in the assassination attempt. So, he sent his lawyer to the Inspector-General Roberto Cruz's office to demand a trial. In the absence of the Inspector-General, his secretary, Benito Guerra Leal met with the lawyer, Arturo Orci. Guerra Leal made note of the situation at one point, saying, "The Pro brothers did not admit any involvement in the plot, and no involvement has ever been proven." Leal promised that there would be a trial the next day.

Within days the newspaper *Excelsior* published an interview with the priest: "Conducted and guarded by the police, the priest, Miguel Agustin Pro was presented to us. 'Are you a priest?' we asked him."

"Yes, sir, a Jesuit priest."

"Do you wish to make a statement?"

"I want to make no statement, except that I am grateful for the attention shown me by those who arrested me. I am absolutely innocent of this affair, because I believe in right order. I am perfectly at peace, and I hope that justice will be served. I deny unequivocally having taken part in the plot [against General Obregón]."

Another paper, *El Universal*, wrote, "When we asked [Fr. Pro] about the crime attributed to him he replied to us, 'I have no connection with revolutionary activities; when justice is done it will be seen that I am speaking the truth.'" Humberto also declared his own innocence. All who knew the Pro brothers were certain that they would never have been part of such an incident. It seems that even Obregón came to realize the brothers had nothing to do with the plot against his life.

Despite all this, Cruz (the Inspector General) had the newspapers report that the Pro brothers had admitted to the crime. It was also reported that Nahum Ruiz, who had been shot and captured on the day of the attempt, had confessed about others taking part in the plot. This, it seems, was another outrageous lie since Ruiz had remained unconscious from the time he was shot in the head until his death a week later!

Cruz was quoted in the newspaper *El Excelsior*, on November 23, as follows:

We were informed in the General Inspection of Police, that the priest, Miguel Agustin Pro Juarez, described as one of the principal authors of the bombing attempt had been eagerly sought for a long time by the agents of the Commissions of Safety. On three occasions he was at the point of being arrested but, we are told, by his cleverness, he succeeded in escaping. And, although great efforts were made by the police to capture him, they proved futile, for he "vanished in smoke" and no one could pick up his trail.

President Calles called in the Inspector-General, Roberto Cruz and told him to execute the Pro brothers as well as the two really guilty of the plot, Vilchis and Tirado. It was to be done without a trial. Cruz suggested it might be prudent to give at least some semblance of legality to this execution. Calles retorted, "I don't want good appearances. I want it done!"

Final Moments

The Pro brothers and others in their company were detained in jail from November 18 until the 23rd. A Chinese gentleman, Antonio Muriozábal, was in the same jail cell with Miguel and Roberto. He wrote about his stay with the two brothers:

I had never seen him before, but I had heard him spoken of frequently. In the two days we were together in the prison I saw him praying for long periods of time and several times daily, by himself. And during the nights we all prayed the Rosary together and sang together the march of St. Ignatius... The dungeon was dark, narrow and unventilated. Despite all this Padre Pro showed great patience, resignation, contentment and even joy. He told us we should be happy to suffer something for Jesus Christ, that if worse evils, even the firing squad, lay ahead for us, we ought to be proud to suffer and die for Christ. I heard him express his own wish to die for Christ... The last night he slept on the floor because he had lent me his mattress.[16]

At 10:20 am on November 23, 1927 the jailer came and called out "Miguel Pro!" The priest got up, put on his coat, and bid goodbye to his fellow prisoners, "Until we meet in heaven, brothers." As the priest walked out of the prison, one policeman asked forgiveness for having been involved in Miguel's capture. The young priest embraced the police officer and said, "Not only do I pardon you, but I am grateful to you, and I will pray for you."

They led Fr. Pro out into the yard where the firing squad was lined up. Calles had invited members of the news media, government officials and photographers to witness the gruesome event. According to some writers, his plan was to bring the priest before the firing squad and have him renounce his faith. The news media would capture this on film and this would shame the Church. His plan failed.

The priest was asked if he had a final request. "Permit me to pray," he answered. He knelt down and took out a crucifix and kissed it. He also took out his rosary. He offered his soul to God. He refused the usual blindfold, and spoke, "Lord, you know I am innocent." He then gave his priestly blessing to all in attendance, including the firing squad, and then said, "May God have mercy on you. May God bless you."

---

[16]Adapted from Frachón Royer, *Padre Pro*, P. J. Kennedy & Sons, pp. 220, 221.

He calmly walked over to the wall, turned and faced the firing squad. He held his arms out as if he were on a cross, and said, "With all my heart I forgive my enemies." As the soldiers were about to shoot, he quietly cried out, "*Viva Cristo Rey!* (Long life Christ the King!).

Then the command was given and the sound of gun shots pierced the air. Padre Miguel Agustin Pro fell to the ground dead. One soldier approached and to be absolutely certain of Fr. Pro's death, fired a bullet into his head. He was just 36 years old.

The execution of Humberto Pro, and two of the men actually involved in the plot took place, one by one, after that of Miguel. Roberto Pro was detained in prison under the sentence of death.

The sister of the two Pro brothers, Ana Maria Pro, having seen the movement at the Inspector-General's headquarters correctly reasoned that her brothers were about to be executed. She begged to see them, to speak to them, but her passionate request was ignored. She had stood in tears outside the compound.

As the bodies were brought to the hospital, people knelt in the street to honor the relics of these martyrs. Ana Maria was the first to view the bodies of her brothers. Shortly after, their father arrived to honor the bodies of his dead sons. He dipped his handkerchief in the blood of Miguel, and kissed the forehead of each of his martyred sons. Ana Maria threw herself into the arms of her father and wept bitterly.

Mr. Pro Told her gently, "There is nothing more to weep over, my child." He thanked God to be the father of two martyrs.

Later, the two bodies were placed in the family home and a steady stream of people came to venerate the bodies of the Pro brothers. From 5 to 11 pm and again the next day from 6 am to 3 pm thousands came to pray and to touch religious articles to the coffins of the two martyrs.

Fr. Alfredo Mendes Medina, a Jesuit who used to bring the Pro sisters with tiny Miguel in his arms to walk the gardens at the Convent of Guadalupe, offered Mass for all those present.

Mr. Pro knelt for hours between the two coffins, placing one hand on each. When he finally stood, he said only, "Miguel was an apostle; Humberto an angel."

That night when Mr. Pro went to lock the doors he found five or six police officers seeking entry into the house. Mr. Pro wrote that this made him uncomfortable, thinking they had come to cause him and his family more grief. "But far from that, they humbly begged to be permitted to visit the bodies, and I consented. They knelt before the bodies and prayed respectfully. When they arose, one of them said to me, 'If there is anything we can do for you, please count on us.'"[17]

Having been told by General Cruz that Roberto would be permitted to come to the house some time that night to see the bodies of

---

[17]Royer, p. 236

his brothers, the priest saved a host so that Roberto could receive Holy Communion. Since Roberto was not granted the promised consolation the priest placed the Blessed Sacrament on Miguel's coffin for all to adore.

At 11 pm Fr. Soto preached a holy hour. Following this Fr. Mendez Medina heard the confession of about fifty people. The rosary was prayed until 4 am, at which time the two priests offered Mass.

The crowds which had gathered were admitted to the house from 6 am to 3 pm as has been mentioned. Many brought crucifixes, rosaries and other religious objects to touch to the bodies of the two martyrs. At 3 pm, the bodies were carried out of the house, and the cry boomed far and wide, "Long live Christ the King!"

Funeral Procession

The funeral procession was huge. Despite the fact that Calles had forbidden any public display of sympathy, there were more than 500 cars in the funeral procession. Flowers were thrown from the balconies along the funeral procession route. The people processing prayed the rosary. By the time they reached the cemetery there were thirty thousand people on hand.

While the procession was passing through the city, the people called out "Long live the martyrs! Long live the Mexican clergy!

Long live the Catholic religion! Long live our bishops and priests! Long live the pope! Lord, if you want martyrs here is our blood!"

A number of priests met the funeral procession at the gate of the cemetery and volunteered to carry the body of their priest friend to the grave and to lower it into the ground. This, of course, was at the risk of their lives.

Despite the president's order that the photographs of the execution not be published, they were printed and distributed across the country and indeed around the world. People who had never heard of Miguel Pro now admired him as a martyr. Within days, he had become the most popular priest in Mexico and he remains so even today.

Miracles

Before his martyrdom, which he seemed to anticipate, he remarked to a friend, "If I am ever caught, be prepared to ask me for things when I am in Heaven." To another friend, he had joked that, if asked to give his life for the faith, he would deal out favors from heaven as if they were a deck of cards.

He kept his promise. In early November, 1927 one of his penitents had come to him concerned about her financial situation. She brought some of her financial records to Fr. Pro and he promised to look them over. He was captured before he could do that.

When she heard of the priest's execution she hurried to see her lawyer and tell him the bad news. The lawyer exclaimed, "That's impossible! Hardly ten minutes ago Fr. Pro himself came here to return your papers."

The day after Miguel's martyrdom, a gentleman known as Don Valladares was speaking to an old woman friend about all the heart-rending events in Mexico City over the death of the young priest. She wanted to go herself but she had been blind for six years. Valladores suggested she pray to Fr. Pro to be healed. She had barely offered her prayer when she grabbed the hand of her friend and thanked him for the advice.

"Can you see?" he asked.

"Yes," she responded.

"Do you know how to read?" asked Valladores, hoping for some proof of her healing.

"I did before," she answered. She took a paper he was holding and began to read it out loud. She was indeed healed.

Upon hearing of the cure, a priest in the area quickly traveled to Mexico City to be present at Fr. Pro's funeral. There, as he stood near the family during the burial, he told them of the miracle he had just observed through the intercession of their martyred son.

Another healing occurred in the case of a Poor Clare nun. In 1925 she fell from a height of fifteen feet while cleaning a bannister. She was unconscious for several hours. She had a fractured spine and several ribs were injured. She endured terrible pain for three years.

In January 1928 someone brought a relic of Fr. Pro and encouraged her to pray to the martyred priest. She did, and as soon as she touched the relic to her body, the pain began to diminish. The next day the pain was completely gone. Shortly thereafter, she got out of bed, dressed herself, and returned to her active life as a healthy sister in her community.

A young woman named Joaquina Delgado y Riestra was diagnosed in mid-July 1927 with breast cancer. Her doctor, Luis Vaszquz, prescribed an operation to remove her breast. She refused, and asked him to recommend an alternative treatment. He sent her for X-ray therapy. She returned two months later and was much worse. She was by then suffering pain in her lung. He told her she had better have the operation and soon.

She visited two other doctors, and both told her an operation was absolutely necessary. In early December (1927) Vasquez was told Joaquina had decided to have the operation. However, she began to pray a novena to Fr. Pro, and touched his relic to her breast. She began to feel better and returned to Dr. Vasquez in mid-December for another diagnosis. He was amazed to see the large ganglions of cancer had almost completely disappeared.

Vasquez examined her one final time December 26. He reported that Joaquina was then in perfect health and showed no signs whatever of the breast cancer he had seen in her. She told him it was due to her prayers to Padre Miguel Pro. The doctor signed a statement confirming all of this on January 4, 1928.

Reports of cures and other miracles began to pour in to El Paso, Texas, where they were recorded. And, the miracles were not limited to Mexico: the conversion of a man in France about to die who had stubbornly refused confession and the last sacraments; the cure of a woman in Spain; the healing of a woman in Rome.

Postlogue

Miguel Agustín Pro was beatified by Pope John Paul II on Sunday morning, 25 September 1988. In his beatification homily, the Holy Father said of Blessed Miguel Pro, "Neither suffering nor serious illness, nor the exhausting ministerial activity, frequently carried out in difficult and dangerous circumstances, could stifle the radiating and contagious joy which he brought to his life for Christ and which nothing could take away. Indeed, the deepest root of self-sacrificing surrender for the lowly was his passionate love for Jesus Christ and his ardent desire to be conformed to Him, even unto death."

The death sentence for Miguel's brother, Roberto Pro never came to pass. His life was spared due to the intervention of the Argentine minister to Mexico, Don Emilio Labougle. He was highly regarded by both Calles and Obregón, despite his being a devout Catholic. He had often attended the Masses of Padre Pro at the invitation of the man who hosted the Masses, his friend, Roberto Nuñez. When the three brothers were captured, Labougle urged restraint from Calles. Calles gave his word that the Pro brothers would be exiled, nothing more.

It seems Calles' word was not worth much, as we have seen. Miguel Pro was shot at 10:30 am, followed by Luis Segura. It was another hour before Humberto Pro and Vilchis would be shot. Nuñez heard of the execution of the first two just after 10:30 and called Labougle. The latter rushed over to Calles to complain over his betrayal. Calles blamed it all on Obregón, which was a bald-faced lie.

To show some good will, Calles called General Cruz who told him, "We're getting ready to kill Roberto Pro." Calles stated, "Well, let that one off. We'll exile him."

Obregón sent his lawyer to complain to Cruz over the execution of the two Pro brothers. He had never believed they were guilty. Cruz sent his answer that only Obregón himself had the power to stop it. He should have spoken up if he had wanted it stopped.

This is said to be the way Roberto Pro was spared from the death penalty, and was banished from Mexico. He went with his father and his sister Ana Maria to live in Cuba for a time, in poverty.

They were permitted to return to Mexico in September 1929. Roberto was about 26 at that point. Some time after their return both Roberto and his sister Ana Maria married well. Mr. Pro, who lived with Roberto and his wife Lolita, died in 1939. Roberto himself died two years later in 1941, clutching the crucifix of his martyred brother

Miguel, and saying the famous words of Mexican believers, "Viva Cristo Rey!" (Long live Christ the King!).

Calles and Obregón

Calles had agreed to hand the presidency back to Obregón in 1928. When other candidates came forward to challenge the Obregón candidacy, they were shot.

Obregón was re-elected president in 1928 but was assassinated himself before he could take office. Calles put his puppets into the presidency and stayed in power behind the scenes until 1934. At that point, another of his friends, Lázaro Cárdenas was elected president, and was expected to carry out the orders of Calles. However, it seems their friendship soured fairly quickly after the election and Calles was exiled to the United States in April 1936.

He remained in San Diego, California until 1941 when Manuel Ávila Camacho, a Catholic, became president. His policy of reconciliation paved the way for Calles' return. Allegedly, upon his return, Calles expressed sorrow over his violent policies when he had been president and added that, "the salvation of Mexico lies in Conservatism and Catholicism."

Calles lived in Mexico City and Cuernavaca until his death in 1945. He was 68 at his death.

Reflection

Miguel Agustin Pro was a happy fun-loving clever priest who lived a fascinating though short life (36 years). He endured exile from his country and from his mother due to the violently anti-Catholic regime in Mexico during his seminary years. He endured his own physical trials with his stomach ailment, including three excruciating operations. Added to that were night after night of sleeplessness. Through it all, he remained jovial and cheerful.

When he was finally able to return to his native land, his grueling schedule of ministry to his people seemed to re-energize him. It appears that his stomach problems left him and he was given a short respite before his final act of self-sacrifice.

His final three words summarized his whole purpose in life: Viva Cristo Rey! May the example of this joyful, energetic martyr inspire each of us to live our faith with a similar joy and abandon. And, may Christ our King reign forever in our lives and in our world!

Sources

Dragon, Antonio, S. J., *Miguel Agustin Pro of The Society of Jesus*, English trans. by Lawrence Drummond, Montreal: The Messenger Press, 1930 pp. 30-216.

Forrest, Rev. M. D., MSC, *The Life of Father Pro*, Lexington, KY: St Pius X Press, 1944, pp. 2-108.

Royer, Fachón, *Padre Pro*, New York, NY: P. J. Kennedy & Sons, 1954, pp. 81-241.

Van Hove, Brian (1994). "Blood-Drenched Altars". *Faith & Reason*. http://www.ewtn.com/library/homelibr/fr94204.txt.

Chapter Five

St. Teresa of Ávila

(1515-1582)

St. Teresa, sometimes known as "the great Teresa" to distinguish her from the Little Flower, was a strong-willed woman. When she gave that will to God she was able to do marvelous things for Him and His Church.

Early Life

Teresa was born in or near Ávila, Spain in 1515, one of twelve children, of whom she wrote, "All, resembled their parents in being virtuous, through the goodness of God, with the exception of myself–although I was the most loved of my father." She said her father and mother were both religious and virtuous. Her father gave her good books to read and her mother taught the children to pray and to love the Blessed Mother and the saints. This "awakened good desires" in her from the age of six or seven.

Her father was kind to the poor and to his servants, and would not hear of keeping slaves as many did at the time. When a slave of his brother stayed with him, he "treated her as if she were one of his children." He was known for being honest; he never swore or criticized others. And, he lived well the virtue of chastity.

Her mother was often sick. She was also "particularly chaste" and modest about her beauty, which was considerable.

At seven Teresa enjoyed reading the lives of the saints, which she shared with her brother Rodrigo, who was four years older. She saw how earthly pleasures seemed to end in tiredness or disgust or lack of interest, but her parents had mentioned that the joys of heaven would go on forever. That thought impressed both Teresa and Rodrigo, prompting them to repeat often together, "Forever, forever, forever... forever."

Teresa decided that the martyrs had found a wonderful way to heaven. So, she got her brother to join her in setting out secretly to Moorish country to be martyred. Captured by an uncle, they were returned to their worried mother who scolded them, whereupon Rodrigo blamed everything on Teresa, perhaps fittingly so.

Constrained by their parents from their true goal, the two decided to become hermits, attempting to build hermitages, but with little success. They would pile stones for the structure but they would come crashing down soon after they began. All of this took place when Teresa was just seven.

Teresa would give alms to the poor, what little she could. She often went off to pray by herself, offering the prayers her mother had taught her. The rosary, a favorite of her mother, became one of her favorites as well. She would get her young friends to join her in acting as if they were sisters in a convent.

Her mother died at the age of 33 when Teresa was just 13. Deeply hurt by this loss, she, in her words, "went before an image of our Lady and asked her with many tears to be my mother." She said that this helped her in that Mary responded well to her requests and brought Teresa close to her.

Teresa and the other children often read romances, which their mother owned and permitted them to read. However, they had to sneak them since her father disapproved. Soon, she and Rodrigo began to write their own–and hers was pretty good. This interest in romances began to take up much of her time and she became attached to it. This turned Teresa from God to the world whereby she began to concern herself with dressing stylishly and with putting on perfume, and other worldly things.

She also was influenced by some of her cousins to think more of the world than of God. There was one particular cousin, whom her mother had unsuccessfully tried to keep from Teresa, who encouraged her in worldly ways and "vanities" as she put it. She noted with some surprise how much damage this friendship did her. In her *Autobiography* she warned parents about the negative effect bad friends could have on children, especially during the teenage years.

She said she later sinned with the servants who were only too happy to spur her on in evil. She was clever about keeping this secret from her father, who thought she was a little angel. However, she knew in her heart she could not keep it secret from God. After three months of misbehavior, her father sent her at 16 to a nearby Augustinian convent to be educated.

Vocation?

There she met a nun who helped her recover her past devotion, and Teresa herself began to think about the possibility of entering religious life, although she was far from ready to commit. However, after 18 months she became quite ill and had to return home.

When she got well she stayed with her sister for awhile, and then for a short time with an uncle who was most devout. He got her to read him books on the saints and on holiness. She did, and even pretended to enjoy them to please him. He spoke to her about God and how unsatisfying the delights of this world are, something she had known when she was younger, but had forgotten. All of this had a good effect on her.

She made herself consider religious life, thinking it would be hard, but not as hard as purgatory. Her thought of becoming a nun was, as she put it, out of fear, not love. Although she was quite right about the hardship of purgatory, she was mistaken in thinking that one who is called to be a nun has a miserable life. Only much later did she come to know the great joy of being a nun. And, of course, she was wrong in thinking that it was her choice, rather than God's.

In any case, with her flawed reasoning, she decided she would join a convent. She told her father of her intention, but he would not hear of it. No one was able to convince him. Fearing she might weaken in her decision, she secretly set out one morning with her brother to enter the Carmelite convent outside Ávila. She said she suffered great interior conflict at disobeying her father. She arrived there in 1535, at the age of twenty.

The Prioress sent a note to Teresa's father to have him come and visit with her since he had not given her permission to join. He went, and surprised everyone by giving his permission!

Teresa was also pleasantly surprised to find her sadness melted away as soon as she arrived at the convent. She was actually happy! And her happiness would continue for the rest of her days. This puzzled her. She wrote later "All the things of religious life delighted me." In any case, it seemed that, though she was unaware of it, she did indeed have a call from God to become a Carmelite nun.

She described herself as handling hardships with great imperfection. When they suggested her tears indicated she was not happy being there, she was angry, but said little. She did not handle rejection well, and wanted everyone to think highly of her. It was only much later she would learn the way of the saints to embrace rejection and shun praise.

When she saw one of the sisters endure terrible suffering with tremendous patience, she was deeply impressed. She prayed that the Lord would send her whatever sicknesses she needed to be close to Him.

She made her profession in 1537, at the age of 22. God, it seems, heard her earlier prayer for sickness, for she became miserably ill once she was professed, and after a short time her father had her brought home, where various quack doctors succeeded in making her worse.

Sickness

During this time a priest who was living in sin came to hear her confession. He was involved with a woman and the whole town seemed to know about it. The woman had given him some charms which he wore around his neck as a symbol of his love for her.

Teresa showed him much kindness, hoping to be able to influence him in the right direction. Eventually, he gave her the charms and she threw them in the river. After this he was cured of his addiction to the woman. He ended the relationship. He died just one year from the time he first came to see Teresa.

During her illness she suffered the shrinking of her nerves, which is just about the most painful one can endure. This lasted for more than two months, but she was given the grace of patience. This surprised her, and impressed her fellow nuns. At one point she had a convulsion and she stayed unconscious for four days. She couldn't feel a thing. All thought she was about to die. They had actually dug her grave at the Convent and prepared for the funeral Mass.

She described her illness during those four days as follows: her tongue was "bitten to pieces"; she couldn't even drink liquids since she had eaten nothing; she had no strength whatever; her bones seemed all out of joint; her head seemed to be all mixed up; she said she was "all shriveled and drawn together in a ball." She was unable to move her limbs; she was so sore that no one could touch her without her experiencing great pain; to move her they had to carry her in a sheet.

She recovered however, enough to be brought back to the convent later in August, 1539. She described herself as no more than a bunch of bones. She endured her paralysis until about April 1542. Realizing the earthly doctors could do nothing, she turned to St. Joseph and asked him to heal her. the nuns also prayed to him and had Masses said for her. Once as she crawled about the convent, the best she could do with her paralysis still affecting her, she sensed she could stand. So she did, and surprisingly, she could! She was able to walk normally, as if all those years of sickness had never happened. The other sisters believed it to be a miracle.

Although St. Joseph had taken care of most of her illness, she was still to suffer some illnesses for sixteen more years. Perhaps this was God's continued answer to her early prayer for suffering whatever was needed to bring her close to Him. Each morning from the age of 24 through 40 she endured nausea and vomiting. She was unable to eat before noon. She endured sharp pains near her heart and, for several years, fevers. Every evening, before retiring, she would vomit as well.

Socializing

Shortly after returning to better health, she began to follow the custom of socializing with the far too numerous visitors who came to the convent. One of the older nuns whom Teresa respected a good deal urged her to cut back on her socializing, but Teresa found her annoying. She felt this woman was all concerned about nothing. She wouldn't hear of changing her behavior.

Then, one day while she was visiting with a new friend, she saw with the "eyes of her soul," Jesus, looking at her very sternly, as if quite unhappy with her conduct. She was quite upset over this and had no desire to meet with that individual again. However, after a while she presumed it was just her imagination.

She thought no more of it and continued to socialize with this same person for some years. She didn't want to give up visiting with this person since she enjoyed it so much. However, she knew in her heart it was at best a waste of time. At worst, it became an attachment, something she felt necessary for her happiness, and an obstacle to becoming truly close to God.

Then, another time both she and her friend and others, saw a large ugly toad moving toward the two of them, at a curiously rapid pace. Again, after a time, she convinced herself it was just her imagination playing tricks on her.

Teresa also began to neglect her private prayer. She told her father that she had not been praying because of her continuing illnesses, while at the same time she was helping him and others get into prayer. She admitted, however, that this was a lame excuse for herself. In fact, it was more due to her excessive attachment to her friends who came to visit. She felt "ashamed" to go to God in mental, i.e., personal, meditative prayer. She said she was "deceived" by the devil to keep from this prayer out of false humility.

Attachment to friends, i.e., loving them for one's own sake rather than for their sake or God's sake, may seem like a small fault, but the obligations of a religious are far more strict than those of a lay person. Detachment, that is, needing only God and whatever gifts he chooses to give for the moment for happiness, and seeing all else as unnecessary, is essential to a holy life. The whole purpose of becoming a religious is to strive for perfection. Teresa and her fellow sisters knew this well.

When her father became ill in late 1543 she joined her brothers and sisters at his side. He suffered from a terrible pain in his shoulders which continued night and day. Teresa suggested that this might be God's way of letting him experience some of what Jesus endured in carrying His cross. (He often meditated on this event.) This consoled him greatly, to the point that he no longer had any complaints about his agony.

Teresa was deeply moved by the death of this holy man on December 24, 1543. Before he passed away, he had told his children to remember that everything in this life will come to an end.

Struggles in Prayer

After he died, she went to confession to her father's spiritual director. When she told him about her slacking off in private prayer, he warned her of the danger of what she was doing and to never give up this prayer again. Immediately she returned to it and never again neglected it. However, she continued on in her sinful attachment to her visitor.

She found it difficult to pray, since it made her see her sins all the more clearly. She later wrote in her Autobiography that whoever begins meditative prayer should never give it up, no matter what his sins might be.

Once she had gotten into prayer again she was always ready to hear a sermon, even if others thought it was bad, because she delighted in speaking of and hearing about God. However, she agonized over the fact that she was not living up to what was being preached. She was caught in the middle, between her love for God and her love for the world, that is, her worldliness. She wanted to move toward God alone, but she could not bring herself to do so. And so, she suffered.

Convinced of her unworthiness, she prayed to King David, St Mary Magdalene and St Augustine, all great converted sinners, for help. She chose them because they had resisted God's grace for some time before surrendering to Him. The difference between them and her, as she saw it, was that when the Lord called them to change their lives they responded, while she had turned a deaf ear to many such calls.

She felt so miserable when it was time to enter the chapel for meditative prayer, she would force herself to go in to pray. She could hardly wait for the hour to be up. Nonetheless, after she made herself do this, she often felt better about her prayer than when she felt like praying! This is typical of many who begin to pray–it is extremely difficult at first to get into the habit, but once a person has gotten through that difficulty, they begin to enjoy prayer, especially when they see what it does for them.

Conversion

In 1554, Teresa entered the chapel and saw there a statue of Jesus covered with wounds. It had been borrowed by the convent for a feast day celebration. Seeing her Lord in such a pitiable state, and how ungrateful she had been for so long, she was moved to throw herself on the floor face down, and let a flood of tears come forth as she begged Jesus to give her the power to stop offending Him.

She told the Lord she would not get up from there until he granted her prayer, and it seemed that He did grant it. She would often think of Jesus' agony in the garden and that she was there to console Him.

She began to be more and more attracted to prayer, and to spend less time chatting with visitors. The other nuns noticed the great changes in her.

She began to advance rapidly in prayer, reaching higher and higher levels. She describes four levels: the first, in which the soul does most of the work, as a gardener fills buckets from a well to water a garden; the second, in which one uses a winch with a crank to raise the bucket and a trench to feed the water to the garden. This she called the prayer of quiet. The third level, is that in which the garden of the soul experiences running water from a spring or river provided by God. Much less effort is needed by the soul for prayer. In this third stage, the faculties (touch, hearing, etc.) are totally fixed on God. Finally comes the fourth level, in which the garden is watered by a good rain from God, and this requires virtually no work by the soul. She called this the prayer of union. It is accompanied by what Teresa called the "most marvelous and gentlest delight." All of this should give us hope, knowing that if and when we progress in prayer it gets easier and easier.

She said she experienced the prayer of quiet at this point, and long periods of the prayer of union. She sought advice about what this wonderful experience meant from two holy and somewhat educated priests. They consulted together and decided that her faults, which she readily admitted, and such favors from God were incompatible. Such "spiritual graces," they declared, are only found in those advanced in virtue and who do many penances." They told her she was being led astray by the Devil. She was crushed. She cried and cried for days.

However, a friend referred her to another priest, a 23-year-old Jesuit, Diego de Cetina, who came and listened to her story. He concluded that these delights at prayer were from God. Nonetheless, he suggested she needed a stronger grounding in the spiritual life, and she needed to practice mortification. She was delighted to receive his guidance.

She began to perform some strong mortifications, including placing some brambles on her bed and rolling around on them, so as to imitate Christ in his sufferings. She also wore a kind of light metal grate which caused wounds in her body. As she continued these things her health, surprisingly, improved. Her morning sickness came to an end, although her evening sickness stayed with her all her life.

Alas, after only four months, Fr. Cetina was moved and Teresa lost her much loved spiritual director. She feared she might fall back into her old ways, but in a short time she found another Jesuit, to guide her, at least temporarily. She had to go out of the convent to see her director. Once while in San Gil to see him, she met a beautiful, devout young widow who would spend many hours before the Blessed Sacrament there, Doña Guiomar de Ulloa.

This woman helped Teresa find another good spiritual director (her own) when her director was transferred, and also got permission for Teresa come to live with her.[18] Teresa stayed there for three years beginning in 1555. This allowed Teresa to visit with her new director often. She made great progress in prayer there, isolated from the 130 nuns in her convent.

Her director, Fr. Juan de Pádranos, insisted that she stop having conversations with certain friends, since she was attached to them. She said it would seem she was ungrateful to stop speaking with those who had been kind to her. He told her to pray to God to find out his will for her regarding these relationships.

Graces from God

She got her answer rather quickly. One day after she had prayed a long time, she went into ecstasy, and heard the Lord say, "From now on I want you no longer to have conversations with men but with angels."

---

[18]Ladies of that era would often invite religious sisters to stay with them, to help them with their religious devotion.

When she regained her consciousness all those nearby were amazed and she was filled with fear. They were all speaking at once, and loudly. "You were like a dead person!" "Your limbs were stiff and your body was ice cold!" "You had no pulse..." She tried to have them think she had fainted, but they were not buying that.

They responded, "We've seen you faint more than once. Your face was not ecstatic as it was this time."

She could barely move. This went on for two or three days. The word got around at her convent and it caused quite a stir. After that died down, Teresa felt a wonderful delight, and had new strength to let go of all her worldly attachments. From that time on, she was only close to people who loved the Lord.

Teresa made new efforts to become holy. She fasted, did painful penances and even wore a hair shirt. This began to have a strong influence over her hostess, Doña Guiomar, who had lived in luxury up to this point. She began to dress humbly, to spend long periods of time on her knees and to treat the poor and lowly with the same good manners she used with the nobility (something no noblewoman did in those days).

Both women were the subject of much gossip in the town. Some saw Teresa as a saint, others doubted her sanctity. People were suspicious of extraordinary gifts since just twelve or so years before a young nun admitted that her ecstasies were faked and her extraordinary gifts were due to a pact she had made with the devil.

The Lord began to appear to her, not that she could see Him with her physical eyes, nor with the eyes of her soul, but she sensed with certainty that He was there. She experienced His presence constantly for two years. Once he showed her his hands, and another time, He appeared in his sacred humanity, "as the risen Christ in all his beauty and majesty."

Once an angel came to her and pierced her heart with a flaming dart. After this she always felt a deep burning within her, leaving her "all on fire with an immense love of God." It was such a sweet pain that she wanted it never to depart, and she felt she could no "longer be satisfied with anything less than God." After she died, her heart was examined and discovered to have been pierced by a sharp object.

The Lord began to lift her off the ground in prayer, even with others present. She tried to prevent it by hanging on to the railing but she could not stop it. Her face glowed brightly. All this occurred during the period between 1558 to 1560, after she had left the house of Doña Guiomar.

People began to talk, thinking she might be possessed. She had a new director at this time and he was not convinced that the Lord's appearances were really Christ. He and five others questioned her about her extraordinary experiences. He told her to stay away from communion for three weeks, and to show the cross and "make horns at him with her fingers" (a sign of scornful disrespect) whenever she saw the apparition.

She obeyed, but felt horrible in doing so. She asked the Lord to forgive her as she "made horns at Him." He responded, "Daughter, you do right to obey." One day Jesus appeared and Teresa held up the crucifix of her rosary, thinking that the devil would disappear if it were he. Jesus took it, held it briefly and then gave it back to her, but now it consisted of four precious stones–far more magnificent than diamonds–instead of the wood it had been made of. The five wounds appeared on this new cross in beautiful detail. Only she was able to see the cross in its new beauty. After this she received more evidence that the Lord was indeed appearing to her.

Shortly thereafter, in 1560, a priest friend of Doña Guiomar came to Ávila to see about founding a monastery there. His name was (St.) Peter of Alcántara, known for his great penances and holiness. He slept only an hour and a half each night, and even that was done sitting. He couldn't lie down anyway since his little room was just 4 ½ feet long. He walked everywhere barefoot, and wore only a poor sackcloth habit with a small cape over that. He wore a shirt made of metal for penance. He would ordinarily eat only every three days, and lived in extreme poverty. And, of course, he was thin as a rail.

Doña Guiomar arranged for Teresa to come and stay with her so she could meet with Peter, that he might evaluate her spiritual journey. Having done so, he assured her that the spirit of God was working in her, and that she had not been led astray by the devil. He told her that she had gone through one of the hardest things, opposition from good people, and that she would surely have more of this to suffer in the future.

Peter promised her he would speak to her spiritual director and another man who was harassing her, and he did. The spiritual director listened and changed his view, the other, a layman, was not so quick to change. Shortly after Peter left, a new trial came upon her, that of losing the presence of God. She even felt that all the visions she had had were just dreams. She felt that all the heresies and problems in the Church were her fault, a "false humility" inspired by the devil.

A priest came to visit her at one point and told her of his shameful mortal sins, one of the most disgusting she had ever heard of. He had never confessed it out of shame, and had not been able to stop committing it. And, he went on saying Mass in the state of mortal sin. Teresa promised to pray for him and get others to do the same.

When he had to return to his home, Teresa promised to write him. In fact, with all the prayers being offered for him, upon receiving her first letter, he went to confession. However, he wrote and told her that his temptations were still very strong, so much so that he felt they were like the torture of being in hell. Teresa got her sisters to pray more, and she offered to endure his sufferings for him. Her prayer was granted: for the next month she endured terrible sufferings at the hand of the devil. Her trials won him freedom from his temptations, and he thanked her greatly.

Teresa often saw devils around her, and once during this month-long trial, they seemed to be choking her. Once holy water was sprinkled all around, she saw many of them being thrown down by the Lord. She came to have no fear of these evil spirits, and said that by ignoring them, they became weaker.

Another time while she was visiting a convent and was praying in ecstasy, she saw a huge battle between devils and angels. She discovered a couple of weeks later that it had to do with a disagreement between some of the prayerful nuns in her convent and those who prayed little. It was a messy conflict.

More than once she saw a great number of devils surrounding her, but she was protected by a globe of light. This, she said, kept them from getting close to her.

At one point she became fearful that her ongoing "favors" from the Lord might become known by others. This, she discovered, was a temptation from the devil. Jesus asked her one day why this bothered her. Only two things could result: either they would criticize her or they would praise Him. In either case she would benefit.

It was around this time that she had an extraordinary vision of hell, which she describes in her Autobiography:

I was at prayer one day when suddenly, without knowing how, I found myself, as I thought, plunged right into hell. I realized it was the Lord's will that I should see the place which the devils had prepared for me and which I had merited for my sins. This happened in the briefest space of time, but, even if I were to live for many years, I believe it would be impossible for me to forget it...

I felt a fire within my soul the nature of which I am utterly incapable of describing. My bodily sufferings were so intolerable that, though in my life I have endured the severest sufferings of this kind—the worst it is possible to endure, the doctors say, such as the shrinking of the nerves during my paralysis...— none of them is of the smallest account by comparison with what I felt then, to say nothing of the knowledge that they would be endless and never-ceasing. And these are nothing by comparison with the agony of my soul, an oppression, a suffocation and an affliction so deeply felt, and with such hopeless and terrible misery that I cannot too strongly describe it... I cannot find words to describe that interior fire and that despair, which is greater than the most grievous torture and pains... any burning on earth is a small matter compared with that fire.

After this she considered every hardship she had to endure in life easy by comparison. She was also filled with a burning desire to save souls from going to hell by her prayer and penances. She considered herself very blessed to have seen this vision.

A New Convent

Soon thereafter Teresa and some others were discussing religious matters in her room when one person remarked at how hard it was to live as a contemplative among so many other sisters. They mused on how nice it must have been in centuries past to live under the older, stricter Rule. One sister proposed in jest that they ought to bring their own convent back to the stricter rule and then establish some new convents with just a few sisters each, under the old rule. They were all amused at the idea.

Someone pointed out they could hardly change things in their convent since they were not in charge. And even if they could, how would they pay for the new houses? One sister offered some property, while Doña Guiomar, who had just arrived for a visit, picked right up on the idea, saying, "I will help you all I can!" Teresa suggested they all pray about it.

They did, and one day after she had received Communion, the Lord spoke to Teresa saying she should work hard to establish a new convent. He said He would bring it about, and St. Joseph would be its patron. He promised the new convent would be "a star shining with great splendor." She was to mention it to her confessor.

She was sure that this had been the Lord speaking to her, but she didn't want to rush into such a big undertaking. This was especially so because she was quite happy in her current convent. However, the

Lord appeared to her several more times to encourage her. So, she obeyed, and told her confessor. He didn't see how she could do it, but he didn't tell her no. He told her she should mention it to her superior. Meanwhile, Doña Guiomar mentioned it to the Carmelite provincial and he liked the idea, and was ready to help them.

They wrote to Peter of Alcántara and he was all for it. Soon, however, word got out in Ávila about the project and the townspeople were not happy. They persecuted both Teresa and Guiomar, thinking it all utter foolishness. It was the subject of much gossip and all sorts of sarcastic remarks. "What was wrong with the convent she was in after all?" One priest even refused absolution to Doña Guiomar unless she promised to give up the project.

Teresa became very stressed out over all the opposition they were receiving, but as she prayed, the Lord urged her not to lose heart. He told her that this trial would show her the misery the saints had endured in founding new orders. He added that her sufferings were only beginning, more than she could ever conceive of, but she was not to lose heart. It seemed that the whole city was against her, including those who were devout.

Teresa's friend, Doña Guiomar, asked the advice of a Dominican priest in Ávila who had an excellent reputation. He asked them to wait eight days for him to think about it. He asked if they follow his advice, no matter what it was, and Teresa agreed. He had already decided while talking to them that their plan was a mistake, but promised to pray about it. He already knew well the total rejection of the idea in the city. One of the townsmen went to see him while he was considering it and warned him not to get involved in such a foolish project.

However, after a week of prayer he changed his mind. He told them he would help. And, he said that if they came upon anyone who thought their project was wrong-headed, they should send them to him. He encouraged them to move ahead with it without any delay. As a result of his support, many in the town changed their mind.

Teresa's friend Doña Guiomar found a small house for the convent, and arranged for them to buy it. At about this time the Provincial withdrew his support. He felt there was not enough money to do it, and too many people were against it. The nuns at Teresa's convent were so insulted by the idea, he wanted to end any "scandal."

Then Teresa's spiritual director wrote her and told her to give it up, as a mere dream. She was deeply hurt by this, since this priest was so close to her, and often consoled her. She hardly knew where to turn. However, the Lord, told her not to worry but to trust. She was to be quiet about it for now. It would happen.

Teresa did as she was told, namely nothing. But, the Dominican priest who had promised to help, Father Ibañez, with Doña Guiomar, wrote to Rome, as the Lord had instructed Teresa to do. They asked for permission from the pope to establish the new convent. The convent would be subject to the local bishop, not the Carmelite

Provincial who was now against the idea. For the next six months or so Teresa kept quiet about the whole thing.

With the installation of a new Jesuit superior, who liked Teresa's idea, her spiritual director, Fr. Alvarez, became more open to it. The Lord encouraged her to bring it up again, and told her to ask her director to meditate on Psalm 91. Once he had done so his doubts disappeared, and he gave her permission to go ahead with it.

Teresa had her sister purchase the tiny house they had found for the new order. Then this sister and her husband moved in, giving the appearance that it was to be their house. In this way they avoided the suspicion of the townspeople while the renovations took place.

Teresa struggled to find the money to fix the house up, but St. Joseph appeared to her once and told her the money would come. When she doubted it was big enough, Jesus told her not to worry, and she saw how it was just big enough.

While they were living there, their five-year-old son was killed when a section of a wall crashed down upon him. They brought the boy to Teresa and she placed him on her lap. She brushed her face against his, and shortly he was alive again. When a friend later asked how all this could have happened, saying, "Sister, how was this? This boy was dead," Teresa smiled but said nothing.

There were many setbacks as they remodeled the house, such as the collapse of yet another wall, this one just completed by the workmen. Teresa urged them not to blame the workmen for bad work, as this was the work of many devils. "Let them build another," she calmly said.

At this point they ran out of money for the project, and Doña Guiomar decided that for such a strong wall to fall, the Lord must be displeased with the whole project. It was time to give up. Teresa's answer? "If it has fallen, raise it up again!"

Doña Guiomar had to ask her mother for more money. When it was slow in coming Teresa reassured her that the money had already been given and would soon arrive. It happened just as she said.

It was at about this time (August 1561) that St. Clare appeared to her and urged her to keep going. She promised she would help. In fact, the Franciscan Poor Clare convent did help Teresa later on. She felt St. Clare also inspired her to live in poverty in the new convent, and that this same saint prayed for them so that all their needs were taken care of, even though they had no regular income.

Then, a few days later, on the feast of the Assumption, she was meditating on all her past sins when the Blessed Mother appeared to her with St. Joseph to give her a bright white robe. She wrote, "I was given to understand that I was now cleansed of my sins." It seems that this means her sins were made up for, and had she died at that moment, she would have gone straight to heaven without having to spend time in purgatory.

Mary told her that she was pleased that Teresa was "serving St. Joseph" and that her new convent would come about and the Lord would be well served there, as would she and St. Joseph. As a sign that this would all happen, Mary gave Teresa a magnificent necklace with a beautiful jeweled cross. This gave her a wonderful peace, she said.

When people became suspicious that the house and Teresa's reform plans were still alive, Teresa worried that someone might tell the Provincial and he would order her under obedience to forget the whole thing. God intervened to prevent this. It seems that a rich noblewoman who lived in Toledo, sixty miles away, Doña Luisa de la Cerda, had lost her husband. She mourned his death so intensely that her health was in danger. As was the custom of the time, she asked the Carmelite Provincial to send her Teresa to cheer her up. The Provincial sent for Teresa to go to visit her and she received the order on Christmas eve, 1561. Teresa didn't want to go, but as she prayed, the Lord told her to go ahead and stay there until the permission from Rome arrived. The devil had planned some trouble for them with the Provincial and this would avoid it. So, off she went.

Doña Luisa Visit

The tales of Teresa's apparitions preceded her, and many of Doña Luisa's friends came hoping to see her in ecstasy. Teresa decided that riches were a bore, and that the rich made themselves "slaves of a thousand things." Her hostess improved a great deal with Teresa's visit, due, it seems to her charm and holiness.

Teresa visited many of the nearby churches, and was able to help a number of people there, including a Dominican priest she had known from Ávila, who had become casual about his prayer. The Lord gave her a message for him, but she was embarrassed to tell him, fearing he would not take it well. So, she wrote it out in a note and handed it to him. The words were so suited to his situation that he was in awe, and realized they must have been from God. He began to pray with such devotion that Teresa was surprised at the quick transformation.

At about this time her brother-in-law died suddenly without getting to confession. The Lord revealed to Teresa while she prayed that the same sudden death would one day come to her sister as well. He wanted Teresa to get her sister ready for her death. She went to see her and urged her to confess often so as to "be prepared" as Jesus urged us to do. Within a few years she did die a sudden death, without the opportunity to receive the sacraments. Happily, she had been to confession just eight days before. It seems that she spent just a short time in purgatory, for just a week later Jesus came to Teresa after Communion and showed her that her sister was entering heaven.

During the time she was visiting Doña Luisa she met any number of important people. These same people would help her with her reform later on.

Also during this time, a holy woman and former Carmelite, María de Jesús, came to visit Teresa because she too was interested in founding a reformed Carmelite convent. And, she already had the permission from Rome. She had stayed with some reformed Carmelites and had learned the rule well. She had already been given a house in Alcalá. She stayed with Teresa there for two weeks, while Teresa jotted down everything she said. One of the things María taught her was how to deal with Rome, a most worthwhile piece of information!

Teresa learned from María that the primitive rule called for the convents to live in poverty, something which delighted her. She wrote to several priests and theologians to get their opinion about doing this in her new convent, but it seems all were against it. They persuaded her. However, when she went to pray, and she considered the poverty of Jesus, she thought being poor would be the better way. She humbly begged the Lord to show her how she could imitate His poverty.

At this point the holy Franciscan, Fr. Peter of Alcántara came to visit Toledo and Teresa convinced Doña Luisa to invite him to visit them. He knew the value of poverty from his own experience, and he urged Teresa to found her reform in poverty. The saintly priest had spoken and that settled it for her. The Lord Himself confirmed that their being poor was the way He wanted.

After six months visiting with Doña Luisa, Teresa received word from her provincial that she could return to Ávila whenever she was ready. She received word from one of the nuns there that they were considering electing her superior of her convent. The very thought of this terrified her.

The Lord told her to go, and that a cross awaited her there. She feared the cross was for her to be elected, but she was mistaken. In any event, she obediently returned home to Ávila, where she would soon begin her life's mission. Doña Luisa was sad to see her go, but go she must. She was 47 years old.

Poverty?

The night she arrived the permission was received from the pope to found the new convent. The same day the bishop of Ávila arrived. This was truly providential since he was the one who had to give permission to begin the new convent without any income. When they asked him he said no, a convent without funding was old-fashioned, and he would not hear of it.

Friar Peter of Alcántara also happened, by God's grace, to be in Ávila at that time. When he heard of the Bishop's refusal, he wrote him a note—since he was too sick at the time to go see him—urging him to accept the convent in poverty. The bishop went off to his country house without even answering this holy priest.

Peter was not to be denied. Sick or not, he traveled the 32 miles to the bishop's house. The bishop was moved by Peter's great interest in this little convent, but the answer was still no. "I won't have poor nuns!" he declared as Peter departed.

After the holy friar left, however, the bishop had a change of heart, perhaps after thinking about Peter's urgings. He sent Peter a message saying that he would consider having the convent without an income and he was going back to Ávila just to meet this "holy nun."

The next day Teresa was told she had a visitor, "the bishop." When he met with her he was "captivated by her simplicity, her sincerity, her quiet intensity... her dignified humility." He was charmed by her strength, her zip. He approved the convent and became her lifelong friend and supporter.

Fr. Peter was delighted with this victory, his last, as he was nearing death. He went off to live his final days in one of his order's monasteries, and died two months later.

The New Convent

Meanwhile, Teresa began to gather her recruits for the new convent, all in secrecy so as to avoid opposition. She chose her first nuns carefully (she had a good eye for sensible, competent women). She sewed the new habits for herself and the other four herself.

Teresa decided to begin the new order on August 24 (1562), the feast of the apostle, St. Bartholomew. He was known as a great protector against the tricks of the devil. She had permission to be in the little house where her sister and her family were still living until the last minute. Teresa had resolved not to go against obedience in any way to establish this new order.

The ceremony, establishing her four novices as "barefoot" (discalced, meaning without sandals, that is, poor) Carmelites, began their opening ceremonies early in the morning to avoid trouble with the townspeople. All was completed by 7 AM. Teresa, delighted that the Blessed Sacrament was now present in the tabernacle, but now exhausted, gave herself to deep prayer for several hours before the tabernacle.

The devil tried to convince her at this point that it was all a big mistake, but she fought him off with a promise to the Lord that she would do all she could to get permission to live there and be cut off from the world. After that she dragged herself off to bed for some desperately needed rest. She had barely had any sleep for days.

She got none. The superior of her convent sent for her to come immediately. She was not happy. The whole town was in an uproar. Mother Superior asked her just what was going on and Teresa explained the whole thing to her. The superior calmed down a bit once she heard from Teresa. Nonetheless, she called in the Provincial and Teresa had to explain herself to him and the whole community. Surprisingly, she was so effective in her explanation that no one found fault with her. The Provincial was pleased with her story that he told her he would give her permission to return to the new convent when the town's anger died down.

The next day the town mayor went with other officials to the house and shouted through the closed door that the city would not accept a new convent, and ordered the four remaining nuns to leave. They were filled with fear at this bold intrusion into their life, but they refused to budge without word from Teresa. The officials threatened to break in the doors, but seeing the tabernacle in the chapel, they pulled back.

Five days later a most solemn meeting was held of the officials and many representatives from religious orders, and one from the bishop as well. The bishop's representative announced that Teresa had permission from both the bishop and the Pope, and then left, no doubt fearing for his own safety! One by one the officials raised their objections to this crazy idea of a crazy nun.

One lone Dominican, Fr. Domingo Bañez, later to become a great theologian, defended Teresa. This humble, holy, 34-year-old priest had never met her, but the whole thing sounded like something that would be most pleasing to God. He was not, however, in favor of founding the convent without an income. In the end, he convinced them all to speak to the bishop, since he was the one responsible, not the city officials.

The bishop defended Teresa. His priest representative told them that he celebrated the opening Mass and reminded them that Teresa had the bishop's approval and the pope's as well. The city officials were not persuaded, but they offered a compromise on September 7:

if the convent were founded with a regular income, they would approve it.

Teresa was tempted to give in. She wrote to Friar Peter of Alcántara who was then dying, and he wrote back telling her to reject the income. Teresa was nonetheless prepared to compromise when Peter, who had just died, appeared to her near the end of October and scolded her for not accepting his advice. The same night Jesus also appeared and told her to reject the endowment. (This should tell us how important poverty is in the eyes of God! Even lay people can and should live more simply.) The next day she refused the compromise and the lawsuit continued.

Finally, the highly regarded Dominican Prior, Fr. Ibáñez arrived in Ávila and when he defended the convent, resistance to it began to wilt. The City Council ruled however that the convent had to be torn down since it was too close to the public fountain and thus overshadowed it. Teresa agreed, as long as they would give her enough money to buy another poor house nearby. The officials accepted her proposal.

Her Provincial delayed her return to her new group until March 1563. In fact, even for him to let her go then she had to plead with him to fulfill his promise. At one point she said, "Father, have you considered that we are resisting the Holy Spirit?" Finally, she was permitted to go, and to bring with her four other nuns from her original convent who wanted to join the reform.

When Teresa arrived, she stretched out, face down on the floor before the Blessed Sacrament. Jesus appeared to her and thanked her for "all she had done for His mother," as he placed a crown on her head.

When she first entered this house which she had founded, she was not the superior. She had named one of the others to that position since she had been given only verbal permission to live there. Even in August she was given permission to stay there for a year by the provincial, in case things did not work out. Having moved there in March, she was not directed to become superior (as was clearly the best thing) until July.

Shortly after she entered that house, as they had just finished night prayer, she saw the Blessed Mother wearing a white mantle, which she held above the nuns symbolizing her protection of this group. From this Teresa realized the wonderful glory the Lord would grant them.

Convent Life

As the townspeople began to see the wonderful prayerful spirit of these humble nuns, all their objections began to fade. In fact, some of their greatest persecutors became their dedicated supporters, and they contributed money for their support. Gradually they let the lawsuit drop, seeing the good that was occurring there.

The nuns would rise daily at 6 a.m., spend an hour in meditation and then pray the Divine Office. Then they would do chores until Mass at 9 a.m.

They had only two meals, one at 11 a.m., the other at sundown. The meals were bland, and there was no meat eaten at the convent, although they were able to find some for the sick when needed. They fasted from September 14 to Easter (excluding Sundays). Meals were silent. Eating between meals was not allowed except by permission.

At two p.m. they prayed Evening Prayer, and then it was time for work, which involved "spinning," that is, making thread. During this work period, one might pray if so moved. At 5 p.m. they prayed night prayer. After that, conversation might be permitted. The evening meal followed, and after that was a recreation hour.

At nine p.m. they prayed the Office of Readings after which they would spend fifteen minutes examining their conscience. Then they would read the passage for the following day's meditation. At eleven they would turn in for the night. In summer the rising, and morning meals were an hour earlier, with provision for a midday siesta.

They slept on a rough bag of straw with only a piece of sackcloth for a cover. There was no glass in the windows, only some canvas attached to a wood frame. This, in a place which could get quite cold–well below freezing–in winter.

The kitchen duty rotated each week among the nuns and when it was Teresa's turn she tried to make everything special. She encouraged the sisters to not become down when they had to leave prayer and take care of kitchen tasks saying, "...don't forget that our Lord is there among the pots and pans!"

The nuns were to practice obedience in all things. At one point Teresa told one of them, who had been quite an elegant lady in the world, to plant a rotten cucumber. The sister asked, "vertically or horizontally?"

"Horizontally," was Teresa's answer. And it was done.

Books

Teresa had been told under obedience to write the story of her life, and she began it in 1561. She thought she had finished it in 1562, but late in that year her director told her to add some things and to revise it all. She finished that, it seems, around December 1565.

It was during this time that she was given many different visions about God and the Church. She saw Jesus one day as if in a mirror, very clearly throughout her whole being. She saw how mortal sin covers over this mirror with a black mist so that we cannot even see the Lord. She saw how heresies in a sense, broke the mirror, and how much more harmful heresy is than the blackening of mortal sin. She spoke in her *Autobiography* about mortal sin:

I saw truly how hell is deserved through only one mortal sin because one cannot understand how dreadfully serious it is to commit this sin before such awesome Majesty and how far from what He is are things of this sort.

At another time she reflected that enduring struggles seemed to be at the heart of life, and she prayed, "Lord, let me suffer or let me die! I don't ask anything else." She was always happy to hear the sound of the clock marking another hour because that meant she was an hour "closer to the vision of God."

The nuns in her convent felt very strongly that their mother superior, Teresa, should write a book on all the things she had taught them about the spiritual life. They presumed she would not write it if they simply asked her–she was too humble for that. So, they asked her spiritual director, Fr. Bañez, and he told her to do it under obedience (which was the sure way to get her to do anything).

So she began writing what would come to be known as *The Way of Perfection*. She wrote this for all Christians, and especially priests, that they might strive for the perfection Jesus said was necessary.[19] This is one of her best books and one of the easiest to read (her writing can be difficult reading at times!).

Lice

---

[19]"You, therefore, must be perfect, as your heavenly Father is perfect." (Mt. 5:48)

The sisters at the convent got word that Pope Pius V was wearing a horse cloth undershirt as a penance. They asked Teresa permission to do the same, and after testing it herself, she approved. All went well until the summer, when the shirts became filled with lice.

These little insects threatened to make prayer virtually impossible, so the nuns formed a small procession walking behind a cross-bearer, singing and praying for relief from these annoying bugs. Teresa heard them and joined in their prayer and songs. They ended in the chapel, where they lay face down on the floor before the tabernacle. Their prayer was so effective that this, and all the other convents Teresa later established were lice-free. They still had the crucifix 400 years later; it was called Christ of the *piojos* (lice).

New Houses

As time went on, more and more young women applied to join her reformed order. Soon she had the maximum number, thirteen, but more kept coming. Teresa felt bad that she could not welcome these applicants, who were some very good women. She received a report from a visiting Franciscan of the millions in America who lived without knowledge of the gospel. Teresa wept at the great need there was for more of her Carmelites to pray for these unfortunate souls.

At one point during her prayer time the Lord spoke to her, "Wait a little while, daughter, and you shall see great things." It was several months before she began to understand what these "great things" might be.

In April 1567 the Superior General of the Carmelites, Fr. Rubeo, came to Ávila and visited Teresa's convent. He found that her group should be under his leadership, not the bishop, and she realized that was the case. He was happy with what he saw there, and when she asked permission to start new convents, he gave it.

She also asked approval for founding a men's branch of the reform, but Rubeo was not so happy about that idea. He refused even a bishop friend whom he was visiting, but when Teresa wrote him a letter saying how Mary would be pleased with a house of reformed friars too, he gave in.

Now she had to find a friar to begin this new house. So, she took it up with the Lord in prayer. She also prayed for a house for the new applicants for her own order.

For her next convent she chose the city Medina del Campo, 75 miles away, because it was large and financially able to support a poor convent. She sent a priest friend, Fr. Julian de Ávila to find a house there, and the Carmelite prior found one and bought it for her, promising that Teresa would pay the woman for it. Fr. Julian went to see it and found it in shambles! The walls were falling in and the place had trash sitting everywhere. He went instead and found another house for her to rent, a nice one, and a rent to match.

Since she had almost no money, it didn't seem to matter what the rent was. Teresa always turned to God for rent money, and He came through. She borrowed some money for the trip and set out on August 12, 1567. About a mile from their half-way stopping place at Arévalo a man approached and told them the rental of the house had fallen through due to the objections of the Augustinians.

A lesser woman would have turned back, but not Teresa. In fact, she was happy to have opposition from the devil, for this meant she was doing something good. She found a place to stay in Arévalo and when the Carmelite prior arrived to try to help her in this bind, he suggested they take the broken down house he had arranged for. Teresa went for the idea, hoping to establish the house on Mary's feast day, August 15.

Teresa got permission from the bishop and then went off to the sad house, arriving after 2 a. m. The place was a disaster, with dirt and falling walls everywhere. Teresa gave everyone a job and she and her sisters began to clean the place, sweeping and washing floors, removing trash and cobwebs, etc. They worked until dawn when all was ready. Argh! Then they discovered they forgot to get the notary to document their new convent. Teresa ran off to get him out of bed and provide the document.

She ran back and had the bell rung and the Carmelite prior offered there the first Mass. It was August 15, the feast of Our Lady.

Teresa was exhausted. When she saw the house in daylight, she saw it was worse than she had thought, and some walls were fallen down, so that the Blessed Sacrament tabernacle could be seen from the street, thereby making it subject to possible abuse. Plus, it was no place for nuns to live. So, a Jesuit priest arranged for them to stay with a noble family down the street for two months while repairs were taking place.

Meanwhile donations began to come in to pay for the house and its repairs. Later, more houses nearby their house were donated as well. What began in a shack was to become something very nice. It all seemed very miraculous.

Some time later she was speaking to Fr. Antonio, the Carmelite prior of Medina, where her new convent was and she told him she had approval from the provincial to start a men's order under the primitive rule. She had been praying that God would provide her with one friar to start it. She asked him if he knew anyone who would be good. He said he did–himself! He had been wanting to live a stricter life, and had already been accepted in the Carthusians.

Teresa didn't think he could endure the rigor of the reform but suggested he prove himself by taking on the penances and strictness of the new order. This he did, and for a year he went through such sufferings and endured such false rumors–all with great patience–that Teresa believed God was preparing him for this new Order.

Shortly after that a newly ordained priest visited her and told her of his holy classmate, Fr. John of St. Matthias. He was living the old strict Carmelite Rule, sleeping just three hours a night, and doing great penances. He spoke of nothing beside God and life with Him. Teresa asked to meet him, and he came.

She discovered he too planned to enter the Carthusians to find a stricter Rule, but she urged him to wait until she could find a house for the reformed Order. He agreed, as long as it wouldn't be too long.

Teresa was delighted with her two friars for the reform. She bounded into the recreation room one day proclaiming, "Blessed be God. I have a friar and a half for founding my monastery!" (John was only five feet two inches tall.)

Her work done, she put one of the sisters in charge of the new convent, and returned home to Ávila. It was the middle of October. Just two weeks later she was offered a ride by friends to go by coach to Alcalá where there was a Carmelite convent in need of her advice. There was also a lady waiting for Teresa to come and establish a new house in Malagón. So, off she went, with two of her nuns.

It took her only a short time to improve things in Alcalá. She had the prioress ease up on the penances which were too strict, and brought back the joy so essential to a convent.

Don Bernardino

On their way to Alcalá, Don Bernardino de Mendoza, the brother of the bishop of Ávila, had given Teresa a very nice house near Valladolid to found a new convent there. While she was at Alcalá

Teresa received news of his death. The Lord told her this man had been in danger of losing his soul but Mary had interceded for him in gratitude for his donating the house for her Order, and he was in purgatory. He would remain there until the first Mass occurred in the house in Valladolid.

She said she was "so conscious of the terrible sufferings of this soul" that she wanted to found the new house as soon as possible, but she had a few more things to take care of in the convent at Alcalá and her friend Doña Luisa was waiting for her to come and found a new convent at Malagón. She went and founded it on April 11, 1568. The city was so small, she agreed to having an income, and the Lord later told her He approved that.

She left that area in late May to return to Ávila, thinking all that time about the need to start the house in Valladolid so that Don Bernardino could be released from purgatory. Meanwhile a relative came and gave her a house in Duruelo to found the house for discalced friars. She had to delay in Ávila for some days and finally left on June 30. She planned to stop and see the house at Duruelo, get John of St. Matthew at Medina del Campo, and bring him to Valladolid to train him while she was founding the house there.

When they got to Duruelo, they found the house to be filthy, and not a decent place for them to stay in. After staying the night in a church, they went on to Medina. She stayed there four weeks, preparing for the two new houses at Duruelo and Valladolid, and training Fr. John. She told Fr. Antonio, one of her volunteers for the men's Order, the house was a mess, but might prove a good house in time. He said he would live with pigs if necessary to found the new Order, and John was just as committed. While in Medina del Campo, as she prayed the Lord urged her to get to Valladolid soon, since Don Bernardino was enduring such agony in purgatory.

So, she left on August 9 for Valladolid to found the house there. The needed permission was delayed, but they did get permission to have a Mass in the house, and so it took place on our Lady's feast, August 15. Thinking that the first Mass of the established convent was needed for the release of Don Bernardino, Teresa was surprised to see him standing next to the priest as she received Communion. He appeared in glory and thanked her for his release from purgatory. She realized that that Mass was satisfactory. In light of the worldly life he led until late in life, Teresa commented, "...our Lord is pleased with any service given to His Mother... For He repays our lowly deeds with eternal life and glory and He makes them great while they are of little value."

Men's Houses and More Convents

In late September she sent John of St. Matthias to Duruelo to start the house there. Meanwhile she began to search for another house at Valladolid, since the location of the house was making all the sisters sick. By the end of 1568 she was planning on a new convent in Toledo. In February they moved to a new house in Valladolid.

In late February she was off to Toledo, by way of Duruelo, where she was deeply moved by the holy chapel John, now called John of the Cross, and Antonio had set up. She arrived in Toledo on March 24, 1569.

She hoped for a quick founding of the new convent but that was not to be. As she had faced before, there was much opposition. They could neither get permission nor find a good house. After two months, Teresa went to see the governor. She explained that it was very sad that a few poor women should have to struggle so hard to live a strict religious life in poverty, while those living luxuriously should hold them back. She convinced him to give the permission.

Now she had permission but no house. One day a poor, young student had come to her and offered to help her in any way. On a hunch, she sent for him and asked him to find her a house for her convent in utmost secrecy, and she had someone to guarantee the rent. Much to her surprise, he did find her a house and she found it quite adequate for a start.

And so start they did, even though they had no furniture but a blanket and two straw mattresses. They started out so very poor, but in time townspeople came to help them. They were a bit sorry to see their poverty taken from them. However, after some time they did indeed live in poverty.

Teresa was very happy with the sisters who lived there, they were so holy. One woman of forty who had health problems and had a comfortable life, sought entry and Teresa accepted her conditionally. Surprisingly, her health improved in her new life of poverty and self-denial.

Two weeks after the house was begun in Toledo, a messenger came from the princess of Eboli inviting her to come and found the house she had promised to found in Pastrana. The princess was going to help her do it. Teresa felt she could not go right away since the Toledo house was so new and in need of her leadership. Nonetheless, she raised the issue with the Lord as she prayed before the Blessed Sacrament for guidance in writing her refusal letter. He told her to go, that she would do more than establish a new house there.

So, she went to see her spiritual director. She explained it all to him without mentioning the message from our Lord. He told her to go, and so she made up her mind to go.

She set out a couple of days later and they stopped on the way in Madrid. She stayed there with some Franciscan nuns who introduced her to a hermit named Mariano who seemed to be living close to the Carmelite Rule Teresa was establishing for men. Teresa spoke to him of this as suggested he might want to join the two men she already had for the reform. (Then she understood what more than the new convent the Lord was speaking of.) After a night of prayer, he was enthusiastic about joining the order.

Mariano had been offered a hermitage in Pastrana by Prince Ruy Gomez (husband of the Princess), and he wanted to use that for the new Order. Teresa was delighted at the thought, and wrote for permission for this second house of reformed friars. Mariano promised to join her in Pastrana when she received permission.

She then traveled on to Pastrana where she had to wait some time while the princess had the house she had bought renovated. After hearing some of the ideas the princess had for the conduct of the new house, Teresa decided they wouldn't do and she decided to leave without founding it. However, the prince convinced his wife to go along with Teresa's plan so she stayed.

Mariano arrived with his hermit friend with the license for the men's house. The prince and princess agreed to allow him to have a Carmelite monastery in the hermitage they had promised him. She sent for two more nuns to found the house at Pastrana, and they came accompanied by a priest. Teresa was delighted to hear that the priest wanted to join the new men's Order.

Meanwhile, the new convent was established there in Pastrana. The prince and princess showed great kindness to the sisters.

Princess of Eboli

Alas, in 1573, when the prince died, the princess entered the house herself as a Carmelite. This was a complete disaster. She arrived in a magnificent coach with her mother and two maids, and enough luggage to sink a ship. She insisted on meeting her friends whenever they came within the cloister rather than behind a grille, and she demanded that her maids be admitted to the Order as well. Finally, the prioress told the princess if she didn't want to follow the Rule, she might be better off elsewhere.

Elsewhere she went, taking for herself one of the hermitages in the garden outside the convent and cutting off the food supply she had been providing for the sisters in retaliation. A devout hermit who came to see the princess warned her she was angering God, but she declared she would be "subject to no one," hardly the best attitude of a Carmelite nun! The day came when Teresa had to move all the nuns (except the princess) to another city!

Still More Convents

Getting back to 1569, Teresa returned to Toledo in July to see about getting a new house and helping the sisters get going. She stayed there a whole year. It was August, 1570 by the time she left to return to Ávila. Once there, she made preparations for yet another convent, this one in Salamanca.

Teresa set out with just one other nun, so as to be able to deal with hardships–and there were always hardships–without other nuns hav-ing to go through that. A friend arranged for them to rent a house which was occupied by students, who promised to leave once the nuns arrived. The trip was miserable: it had rained for several days, and the roads were all mud. At night it turned very cold. To add to all this, Teresa had a toothache and her cheek was swollen. Nonetheless, they made the 60 mile journey in two days and got to Salamanca on October 31, 1570.

When they arrived, they discovered the students didn't want to leave. They had to get the owner to insist that they leave, and they finally did. Not surprisingly, they left the place a mess so Teresa, her companion, and two Jesuit volunteers set about cleaning it up. She sent one Jesuit off to find a carpenter to make the needed changes, and he found one at 8 pm. And, he came!

He worked until 4 am and did four days of work in eight hours. Despite this, he claimed he had plenty of energy when he finished!

At dawn, the familiar bell rang, and they had their first Mass. Poor Teresa had not slept in two days, she went all day cleaning up and then went to bed exhausted. When sister María asked her what she would do if she should die that night and leave Teresa all alone, Teresa replied tersely, "Sister, when that happens I will decide. Now, let me sleep."

With all the foundations she was making, some quoted St. Paul to her, that it was not right for a woman to do such things. She complained about this to the Lord and he answered, "Tell them not to be guided by one part of Scripture but to consider the others as well. Do they think they can tie my hands?"

In late 1570 she was invited to found a new convent in Alba de Tormes. At first she was against it since the town was too small to support a poor convent, but a priest friend told her it would work. So she started off for Alba de Tormes in January 1571 with two other sisters. Two other sisters met them there and John of the Cross came to help renovate the house they were given. The first Mass was said there on January 25, 1571.

Provincial Trouble

She stayed only until March, when she returned to Salamanca to help the sisters there through some difficult times. She left Salamanca in April to go to Medina del Campo to try to resolve a conflict at the convent there. Alas, she sided with her nuns whereas the provincial, Fr. Angel sided with some relatives of one of the nuns who were trying to get back her dowry. Fr. Angel, it seems could not cope with being opposed by this poor nun so he tried to get back at her by naming a nun who was not even in the reformed order to head the Medina convent. She was a good sister, but had no clue about leadership and had tried to become a discalced before at Medina but couldn't take the hard life there.

The nuns at Medina held their own election as their laws called for, and re-elected Teresa's cousin, Mother Inés, who was a wonderful leader. When Fr. Angel heard of this, he ordered both Teresa and Mother Inés to go back to Ávila immediately. Even though Mother Inés was quite sick, out of obedience they left that cold evening for Ávila. The two arrived in Ávila after two days on mules and Teresa went to St. Joseph's convent. She was delighted to be back there without any worries of starting new convents.

In the spring of 1571 Fr. Pedro Fernández came to visit Teresa. He was sent by Pope Pius V to reform the convents in Spain. He was impressed by Teresa, and she by him, as being truly holy. He went on to visit the Medina convent and found the nuns quite miserable, since Fr. Angel's choice of prioress was such a terrible mistake. He sent the prioress back to Ávila and made Teresa take her place.

Superior at Her First Convent

This worked out well, but was short-lived. In July Fr. Fernández attended a large meeting of Carmelites and decided to order Teresa to leave Medina and return to Ávila to be the prioress there. Alas, she was not to be prioress of her St. Joseph's convent, which would have made much sense, but at the Incarnation convent, which she had left years before. It seems that Fr. Angel had incited this bizarre scheme because his choice for prioress was overlooked at the Incarnation and he was still angry over the Medina conflict. This was his way to stir up trouble in both places and keep Teresa from founding any more convents for her three-year term at the Incarnation.

Teresa did not hurry to leave Medina for Ávila. In fact, as she prayed for her brother in Medina one day, the Lord changed the subject and told her, "O daughter, daughter, those in the Incarnation are my sisters, and yet you delay! Take courage and remember that I want it; it is not as difficult as you suppose. Resist no longer for My power is great!"

She set out on the 60 mile journey that cold night. She stayed for a short time at her discalced convent in Ávila until it was time for her to take her new position at the Incarnation convent. She went to the Incarnation on October 6, 1571 with Fr. Angel, the provincial (who caused this mess), leading the way. Teresa carried a statue of St. Joseph.

Fr. Angel sat in the prioress' chair and read the decree from the papal representative making her prioress. When he finished a huge uproar of complaining yells came from the 130 sisters gathered there. Some of the nuns fainted over all this. Teresa placed her hands on the heads of each and each was restored to consciousness. Fr. Angel was frustrated by all this and asked, "In short, you won't have Mother Teresa of Jesus?"

The chorus of nos was pierced by one dissenting voice, "We want her and we love her!" This encouraged the other fearful sisters who favored Teresa to come forward and form a procession behind a crucifix and Teresa as the rules called for. The nay sayers were not to be denied, as they began to curse poor Teresa, and then began to fight the supporters with their fists. All this in a Carmelite convent–such a scandal! They had to bring in the police to bring peace to this awful scene!

Once the police calmed things down, Teresa's supporters gained strength and the procession led her in. The new prioress walked calmly in with her statue of St. Joseph. This was a minor victory for Fr. Angel and Teresa, but the next day would be another test, when there would be a major meeting there.

Her opponents held several secret meetings that night planning how they would thwart Teresa's taking office. They even spoke of physically throwing her out of the convent if necessary.

But, they were no match for Teresa's genuine humility and sincerity. She entered the chapter meeting and without thinking, went to her old seat where she had sat for 27 years. She let out a small chuckle at her mistake, and this cut the tension a bit. She went and got a beautiful picture of Mary and placed it in the prioress' seat.

She began by saying, "Ladies, here is your prioress: Our Lady of Mercy..." She went on to say she had come out of obedience to be prioress against her will and thought she was undeserving. All of this saddened her, she said, because she didn't know what to do and because they were not able to choose their own prioress. "I come only to serve you and please you in all I can... Don't fear my Rule for though I have been living with the Discalced, I think I know, by the grace of God, how one should live [under your Rule]. My desire is that we all serve the Lord quietly..." This little speech won the day. She was accepted.

The new prioress saw quickly that at the heart of this convent's decline was a terrible lack of food. For five years their only food was a portion of bread; for the rest, they were on their own. Many just went home to get food. Sometimes they would spend a month or more with family or some rich friends so they could eat. A major reason they welcomed so many visitors was that they brought the sisters good things to eat.

Teresa attacked the hunger problem right away. She sought help everywhere she could to feed the sisters, and she found a way to pay all the convent's debts, which were considerable. She brought in another discalced sister who had also been at the Incarnation before to help her as sub-prioress.

In Lent she forbade all visitors, something the sisters seemed to bear better than the visitors. One man brought some friends to protest this policy to the prioress. Teresa met him behind the grille. She listened to his ranting and raving, and when he was finished, said, "In the future your Grace will leave this convent [alone] in peace. If your Grace persists I shall appeal to the king."

He went back to his friends a defeated man. This story was spread throughout the town, and most were delighted to hear it.

Little by little Teresa reformed the place. And, little by little the nuns came to like their detachment from worldly things so as to become better attached to God. This was especially true of many who had been rebels at the outset.

Teresa continued with Our Lady of Mercy in the prioress' seat and St. Joseph in the sub-prioress'. The sisters complained that the sub-prioress (St. Joseph) told all their faults to Mary, but with great results. The sisters became so holy that Mary appeared there one day, surrounded by angels.

One of the things that helped them become holy was that Teresa brought in John of the Cross to be spiritual director for the whole convent. She told her sisters she was bringing them a saint as confessor. He warned them against seeking consolations in prayer, saying that such desire was a weakness. He was gracefully strict with the sisters, but with Teresa he was more strict. And, she loved it!

One day (November 12, 1572) John broke the host in half to give Teresa Communion, and though before this might have bothered her as some sort of negative symbolic act, Jesus assured her it was unimportant. Then, He appeared to her and told her "...you will be my bride from today on. Until now you have not merited this; from now on you shall look to my honor not only as creator and King and God, but as my true bride. My honor is yours and yours, mine." This "spiritual marriage" is said to be the highest state one can reach in the spiritual life.

For some time after she seemed to be under a divine spell. She felt she could hardly bear this precious gift, and asked the Lord to "raise her up" to be able to bear it. For the rest of the day she felt drunk with God's love.

The Value of Suffering

On another day, perhaps in that same year, Jesus appeared to Teresa and told her:

Do you believe, My daughter, that there is merit in enjoyment? No, rather it is found in working, suffering and loving. Haven't you heard that St. Paul rejoiced in heavenly joys just once and he suffered often. Look at my whole life filled with suffering and only at Mount Tabor do you hear of my joy. When you see My Mother holding Me in her arms, don't think that she enjoyed those consolations without heavy Torment... The great saints who lived in deserts, since they were guided by God, performed severe penances; and besides this they waged great battle with the devil and with themselves. They spent long periods without any spiritual consolation. Believe me daughter, My Father gives greater struggles to those He loves more... How can I show you greater love than desiring for you what I have desired for myself? ...Suffering is the way of truth...

Hearing this, she said, gave her great joy, and drove out the headache she had when she started praying that day. She wrote that from then on she had "a great desire for suffering."

It was about this time that the Princess of Eboli was asked to leave the convent in Pastrana as mentioned before. When she cut off the funds for the sisters, Teresa went to Segovia to found a convent there and prepare to bring the nuns from Pastrana there. When they got there they established the house and placed the Blessed Sacrament in the tabernacle.

Unfortunately, the bishop who had given permission for the new convent was not in town, and his assistant was furious when he came and discovered it had begun. Teresa was not intimidated by his anger and calmly explained she had verbal permission from his boss, the bishop. (She had learned how to be calm in the most violent storms.) To save face, he left a guard there to make sure they didn't have another Mass until he spoke to the bishop.

Teresa sent a couple of men off to Pastrana to rescue the nuns there and secretly bring them to Segovia so as to avoid the wrath of the Princess. They arrived a few days later in early April, 1574.

The princess was not to be denied her trouble making. She had gotten a copy of Teresa's *Autobiography* and now she sent it to the Inquisition, claiming it contained bad theology. Teresa would only hear of this in 1575.

On October 6, 1574 Teresa was almost unanimously reelected as prioress at the Incarnation. Nonetheless, the Provincial had her instead return to her reformed convent, St. Joseph's and she was elected prioress there a week or so later.

Beas Foundation

In February, 1575 Teresa went at the request of two noblewomen to found a house in Beas, Spain. This was the furthest she had ever gone to start a convent. On the way, they took a wrong turn in the mountains so they prayed to St Joseph and a voice from the ravine below told them to back up and go another way. Was it St. Joseph himself? Teresa knew it was. Later, as they prepared to cross a river, they looked up to see they were already on the other side. There was no denying that miracle!

Word of the miracle(s) got to Beas ahead of them and by the time they arrived, a huge procession of priests and townspeople came out to welcome them. They led them into the Church singing the festive hymn, the *Te Deum*. It was a happy moment!

Another event which allegedly had happened on the way to Beas was one day, presumably a feast day, Teresa was discovered by the cook eating partridge, an expensive delicacy. The cook was surprised, thinking the holy nun should be doing penance, rather than eating richly. Teresa's reply was, "When I do penance, I do penance; when I eat partridge, I eat partridge." Nice answer, Teresa.

The Beas convent was established in the house formerly occupied by one of the parish priests. They could join the parish in prayer through a small window. A parishioner, Alonso de Montalvo, was against this and went to Madrid to take legal action against it. He returned triumphantly saying, "The window will be closed in three days or my eyes will be closed." Alas, the latter happened: three days later he died.

The new convent became a saint factory. Teresa delighted in her stay there among such holy nuns.

She had to stay there longer than expected, since she had to wait for permission to start her next house in Caravaca. While in Beas Fr. Jerónimo Gracián of the Mother of God came to see her. He had joined the men's branch of her discalced Carmelites two years before. He was described as being bright, warmly joyful, very polite, and of a good and cheerful disposition. He also had the art of convincing speech and performed considerable penances. They became great friends quickly and she saw in him someone of great potential for her Order.

In fact, the Lord appeared to her once and placed her hand in that of Fr. Gracián, indicating that they would work together. He was provincial in the Order, and she obeyed him perfectly, as she obeyed all her superiors.

Madrid or Seville

Her obedience was to be tested soon after they met. She was trying to figure out whether to found her next convent in Madrid or Seville. Fr. Gracián told her to ask the Lord in prayer. The Lord told her to go to Madrid. When she spoke to Gracián again, he ordered her to go to Seville. She obeyed Gracián.

He later discovered what the Lord had said to her and asked why she obeyed him rather than the Lord. She answered, "Faith tells me what you commanded is the will of God, but I have no assurance that revelations are..." Some time later the Lord appeared to her and told her she had done the right thing, so important was her virtue of obedience to her superiors. He told her he now wanted her to go to Seville.

So, off she went to Seville, where the bishop had already approved of her new convent-to-be. Before she left, she got word from the Bishop of Ávila that the Inquisition was looking for her *Autobiography*, in that someone (the princess of Eboli) had reported her to them. Teresa's friend, Fr. Bañez wrote some words of approval, and sent his copy of the book to the inquisitors himself. Teresa was her usual calm self. She had learned to trust. Also, the Blessed Mother told her not to worry, that she, Mary had made this cause her own.

She anticipated great trials in Seville. She brought seven sisters with her, and three men, two from the Discalced friars. It was May 18 when they left.

After an eventful trip during which Teresa got sick with a fever, and they had hardly anything to eat for three days, they arrived at Seville. They expected a lovely house and some good food, as was promised. Alas, it was not so lovely and there was no food. There were a few plates, a frying pan and an oil lamp, borrowed from neighbors. Soon after their arrival the neighbors came to get back these things they had lent them. One of the priests that came with them was able to borrow some money and they ate bread and apples for several days, and not much of these. They joked about the hardships.

Shortly they discovered that Fr. Mariano, who said he had the bishop's permission, did not tell them everything. This bishop never approved new convents, and certainly none without an income! He expected the nuns to spread out among the convents already there and help them reform. Teresa was thinking of leaving there and founding a house elsewhere, but Fr. Mariano urged her to stay and he would fix everything a little at a time. Surprisingly, the bishop did warm up enough to visit the house, and was so impressed by Teresa and her sisters, that he gave permission for the convent.

Eventually some local people began to provide them with food and other supplies. Teresa remained there with her new convent for about a year.

Trouble

It was during this time that terrible trouble began to brew for her reformed Order. It seems that a general meeting of the Carmelites was held May 21, 1575 and at the meeting all sorts of erroneous reports of misbehavior by the Discalced Carmelites were voiced. The one person who could have corrected all this arrived late, after the meeting had ended.

The result was not good. They decided to end the three reformed mens' houses of the Order in their area and that all the friars there had to leave. Teresa would not be permitted to start any new houses and was to choose one house and stay there permanently.

Teresa urged Fr. Gracián to go along with the leaders for now until things could be straightened out. Unfortunately, the priests in these houses refused to go along with the decrees of the general meeting, and Gracián had to be their representative in defying the leaders.

When he went to Seville in November, he discovered some of the Calced Carmelites were spreading untrue rumors about him. The worst of these was that his relationship with Teresa was sinful.

Teresa heard of this and although she was beyond worrying about herself (after all she had been through), she was upset that her dear friend Fr. Gracián had to endure this. She heard that he had gone to the Calced Carmelites to fulfill his mission as Papal visitor to the monastery and they had locked him out. Then she heard he had been killed. She threw herself into prayer, and the Lord spoke to her saying, "O woman of little faith. Be quiet. All will be well." Gracián was alive and well.

She was able to get a house started in Caravaca and to move the nuns in Seville to a much better house, with the help of her rich brother Lorenzo. Once the new Seville house was established, she had to go to a house which she could choose, and stay there permanently. So, she went to Toledo. She was happy to go, to be with Jesus, to think only of Him and not to worry about any more foundations. The journey was pleasant and even her health was good!

All of a sudden her life was very quiet, and she loved it. There was much time to pray and this made her very happy. Though she had founded the new Order, she was not the superior of the convent, so she humbly carried out her duties in complete obedience, always with a smile on her face.

Fr. Gracián directed her to finish her book on the foundations (of new convents) and she did so in November 1576. Some time after, as he was discussing a spiritual matter with Teresa, she mentioned that it was covered in her *Autobiography*, but that was in the hands of the Inquisition. So, he directed her to write another book covering that point and some others on the spiritual life. And so she came to write the *Interior Castle*, another of her classic works, which is still in print. She said the Lord showed her what to write in the book, and she finished in just five months. One of the nuns saw her writing the book with superhuman speed as beams of light came forth from her face.

In this book Teresa warns people not to strive for the impossible, but strive hard for the good things we can do. She wrote, "The Lord does not look so much at the greatness of our works, but the love with which we do them."

In August 1577 a new Papal Nuncio (representative) came to Spain, and unfortunately he had no love for Teresa and her reform movement. At about this time a leaflet appeared accusing Teresa and Fr. Gracián of all sorts of immoral activities. Alas, it was written by one of the reformed friars and a lay brother of the order. It was a shameful betrayal.

More trouble brewed when the sisters at the (unreformed) Incarnation convent in Ávila (Teresa's original, which she had reformed), elected her as prioress. The Provincial of the Calced Order in Castile was sent there to undo this election, which was certainly not something Teresa had wanted. He threatened them all with excommunication but 55 persisted in voting for Teresa. He cursed and excommunicated them one by one as he counted their votes and burned them in an outburst of anger. He arranged for another to be elected in violation of their rules. King Phillip had to step in to get the nuns reinstated.

John Jailed

Then, John of the Cross was arrested Dec. 3, 1577 by the Calced Carmelites and put in their prison. John had been ordered to leave the

Incarnation where he was spiritual director and go to one of the Discalced Monasteries. He had refused since he had not received formal notice that his time there was at an end. This was seen as disobedience by the Calced group and so they whipped him and placed him in a dark dungeon (the punishment called for in the Rule for disobedient friars).

Teresa heard about this the next day and wrote to the king for help. King Phillip called for her to come and meet him, so off she went. He promised to help her and she returned to Ávila, to her St. Joseph convent to await his action. It was slow in coming.

Meanwhile on Christmas eve she fell down a flight of stairs and broke her left arm. A quack doctor delayed a month before he came to break and reset the arm (badly), causing her terrible pain. This gave her some motion in her hand, but she could hardly use it and for the rest of her life could not even dress herself without help.

In March, she had heard nothing of any intervention by the king. She wrote Fr. Gracián regarding John, "I worry much about John, lest they bring some other charge against him. God treats His friends terribly; yet He does them no wrong, for he dealt the same way with His Son." To one of her prioresses she wrote, "If you are going to enjoy the Crucified, you have to bear a cross... those whom His Majesty loves he treats like His Son."

John suffered 9 months in his 6' x 10' dungeon, with only a tiny window providing him light to read his breviary standing on a stool.

Here in the darkness, he composed his wonderful poems on the spiritual life, memorizing as he went for lack of paper. These poems are found in his magnificent book, the *Spiritual Canticle*.

On August 15, Mary appeared to him and gave him detailed instructions on how to break free from his prison. He did indeed escape from his cell, with miraculous help from our Lady. He hid for a while in the infirmary of a Discalced convent for some time. He was so thin and weak, he needed it.

Rogue Election

Then we went back to Ávila, and soon after arrived in Almodóvar in time for a general meeting of the Discalced Carmelites headed by Fr. Gracián. It was October 1578. When Gracián held an election, contrary to Carmelite law and opposed by Teresa, John protested. It was all in vain. Gracián went ahead.

When the papal Nuncio, Bishop Phillip Sega, heard of the election, he was in a rage, and he declared the election invalid. He combined the Discalced friars in with the Calced, thereby trying to end the men's reform movement. Gracián was excommunicated for his disobedience and soon after was imprisoned by Sega. Teresa heard of this the day before Christmas in a letter from Gracián, and fearing the end of her reform movement, wept all day and into the night.

But, that evening, before midnight Mass, Jesus appeared to her and actually fed her a light meal the sisters insisted she eat. He said to her, "Daughter, eat. I see how many sufferings you are enduring... Take heart; it is nothing..."

On December 27 Teresa heard that Gracián and one other friar were to be released from prison. On the night of March 18, the eve before St. Joseph's feast, the Lord appeared to her and told her she would be able to leave her convent in three weeks and King Phillip would help them save the reform.

The King Intervenes

When a royal official insulted Sega, he sought an apology by appealing to the king. When the king met with him, he promised an apology from the official, but expressed his anger over his handling of the Carmelites in the strongest possible way. Sega agreed to have four reputable priests to help him investigate the Discalced Carmelites. After some heated meetings with the king, Sega finally came to see that his opinion was based on wrong information. He realized his mistake, and moved to correct it.

On April 1, 1579 Sega freed the Discalced Carmelites from being subject to the Calced and placed over them Fr. Ángel de Salazar, who, although a Calced himself, was a supporter of Teresa and the Reform. This was a huge relief to all the Reformed.

On April 26 the four advisors declared in favor of separating the

Discalced into a separate Province from the Calced. Sega added his name to that on July 3 as they asked the King to seek permission for this. In June a year later the Pope would approve this change.

Non-stop Activity

Meanwhile, Sega made it possible for Teresa to leave the convent where she was and to visit her other convents to make sure they were on the right track. So, off she went to Malagón, then Valladolid, and then Salamanca where she stayed from August through October to correct some problems. Then she went back to Ávila in November, where at the original St. Joseph's convent, she had a heart attack. (Not surprising!) Barely over that, she went back to Malagón to correct some problems she had seen before.

A wealthy lady had promised to build a new house for them there, as the other was too noisy, and when Teresa got there Nov. 25th it was far from finished. She was told it would take six months to complete the building. She told the workmen they could have 13 days, since she planned to move in December 8th, Mary's feast day. Then, she got a broom and started herself to clean the place up. She inspired the workmen to move most quickly and she was given good health (despite being 64, and in her words, "an old hag") until the house opened. And, open it did, on December 8! After this her fever and other problems came back.

In February she went to Villanueva de la Jara to begin a new house there. Large crowds came out to meet her along the way and for this trip she was in great health. A huge procession led her into the city to found the new house. Miracles began to happen in that house, including a multiplication of wheat, when they could afford just 1/10 of the usual.

In late March she was sick again, but had to leave for Toledo to report to the Inquisition which was investigating her *Autobiography*. She got there March 25 and the Archbishop reviewing her book told her there was no need for concern. The book was fine.

In June she set out and visited Villanueva, Medina, Valladolid, and Segovia, staying in inns that were extremely hot and stuffy. While at Segovia, she learned of her brother Lorenzo's death, when in a vision she saw him die, spend a short time in purgatory, and then enter heaven. Less than a week later she saw him at Mass, standing next to the priest and St. Joseph. Upon the death of a holy Jesuit a month later, whom she saw in heaven, she wrote to a friend, "Life passes so quickly that we ought to think more of how to die than how to live."

She visited Ávila and Medina before returning to Valladolid in August, where she caught a terrible flu that was spreading at the time. It looked as if she would die from it. Whereas before she had never looked her age, as she began to recover, she finally looked like a 65-year-old woman. She slowly got better and it was Christmas before she began to feel herself again.

About this time she resolved to found two new convents, one in Palencia, the other in Burgos. Actually, she needed help in resolving this. She had hesitated to do as Fr. Angel had directed her, feeling too sick to do so. However, Jesus spoke to her after Communion one day, saying, "What are you afraid of? ...Do not fail to make these two foundations."

She arrived in Palencia with five sisters and one lay sister on December 29, and unlike so many previous foundations, everything was ready for them. Beds were made up and food and other supplies were in place! And, the people there were *very* helpful to the sisters. It's a good thing, because Teresa was exhausted when they arrived.

That house was rented, so they found another house which had been a place of sin, but which the Lord told her was His choice. The nuns could make reparation for all the sins that had been committed there.

While there Teresa heard the news that the Pope had made the Discalced a separate province. When this took place, John of the Cross was able to make several new foundations for the men's Order. At this time her reform movement had 22 convents and friaries, two hundred nuns and three hundred friars. Things were looking up!

Then she was offered another house in Soria, so off she went in June 1581with seven sisters. This house too was in good order and the foundation took place with relative ease. Having set things in order there, she set out to return to Ávila.

Once she arrived at her original convent, St. Joseph's, she found things to be a mess. There was not enough to eat, the buildings were falling apart, and they owed money to everyone. The priest chaplain had relaxed almost every rule for the nuns, and this was at the heart of the decline. Certain that she could straighten things out, the sisters elected her prioress over her protests.

Once she set the prayer and penance in order, the food arrived, by the grace of God. The chaplain wasn't so happy about her reforms, but that did not hold Teresa back. In a couple of months devotion and order were restored.

John of the Cross came to visit November 7 and begged her to found a convent in Granada, where he was the prior of a men's Carmelite house. The city was so evil, he thought a Discalced convent might help reform it. Teresa turned him down, since she had to go to Burgos and found a convent there. Nonetheless, when he left, she sent two sisters with him to found a new house in Granada. They got there January 21 and the archbishop refused to let them have a house there. But when a bolt of lightening lit his library on fire, and knocked him from his bed, he feared this might be God's way of telling him to accept the new convent. He gave in.

Jesus Intervenes

Meanwhile Teresa was back in Ávila thinking that perhaps it was too cold in Burgos to found a house there, especially with all her illnesses. She decided not to go, but the Lord spoke to her: "Don't mind the cold. I am the true warmth. Satan is using all his strength to prevent the foundation: exert yourself for me that it may be made, and go in person, for great good will come of it." So, off she went to Burgos.

It was cold, muddy and snowing when they set out. They sent someone out to see if the way ahead was flooded. Jesus told her, "You can go. Don't be afraid; I will be with you." So, she set out.

Along the way they often got stuck in the mud. The danger increased as they went on. At one point she saw one of the wagons tip over with the sisters about to be dumped in the water when a boy grabbed one of the wheels, with seemingly superhuman strength, and held on until others came to right the wagon. After this, Teresa moved her wagon to the front, saying that she wanted to be the first to drown if that was their fate. To make matters worse, the inn they found for the night had no beds for them.

When they got close to Burgos, there was one more difficult river to cross–very much flooded–over some pontoon bridges that were barely wide enough for the wagons. Fearing death, the sisters all went to confession to Fr. Gracián and another priest traveling with them. Teresa told them as she got in the first wagon, they should go back to the inn if she drowned there.

As she got near the other side of the river, her cart stopped and she jumped out into the knee-deep wintry-cold water. She got somewhat injured in the jump and she cried out, "Lord, amid so many difficulties, this comes too?"

She heard the Lord respond, "This is how I treat my friends."

She replied in frustration and mischievously, "Ah, my Lord, no wonder you have so few!"

To the surprise of all but Teresa, they passed over safely. It was January 26 when they arrived, cold and wet.

Meanwhile Teresa had suffered a sore throat since they had left Palencia. With the difficult journey in the cold and wet, it had gotten so much worse that she could not move her tongue or even swallow food. The day before they arrived at Burgos, her tongue was healed, when she received Communion, but her fever was not. She was so frozen by the cold, damp weather that when she entered the house where they stayed, even a hot fireplace could not warm her up.

Alas, the smoke from the fire made her so sick that she suffered a dizzy spell and she vomited up blood. This latter was so severe that she blew a hole in her throat, a wound which stayed with her for some time. The next day she was so sick that she could not move from her bed.

She was happy to learn, however, that the house their sponsor had bought for them was quite nice. All they needed was formal permission from the bishop, who had already indicated to the bishop of Palencia that he was in favor of the convent. However, when Fr.

Gracián went to the bishop he was turned down. He expected Teresa to come alone and negotiate with him, not bring along the sisters. He would not even allow them to have Mass there, so they couldn't attend weekday Mass. This continued for three weeks.

Once Teresa got a bit better, she went to visit him herself. He was polite, but would not budge. Both she and Fr. Gracián were tempted to give up and return home. But, the Lord spoke to her, "Now Teresa, hold on." She needed this support, as this, her seventeenth foundation, proved to be the most difficult.

Shortly she discovered what was probably the snag in this project: The woman who provided the house had already offered it to another order and now was feeling guilty to have given it instead to Teresa and her Carmelites. Learning this, Teresa quickly gave her the house back and found a couple of small, cold rooms in a hospital to stay temporarily. They moved in February 23, and were happy that even though the place was kind of eerie, at least they had Mass daily and could pray before the Blessed Sacrament. They offered up tons of prayers, asking St. Joseph to get them a good place by his feast day, March 19.

On March 18 Teresa came upon a good house, but the price was much too high. She prayed about it and Jesus said to her, "Are you holding back because of money?" So she bought it, and when others heard of the sale, they tried to get it for more than Teresa had paid. But the deal had been sealed.

The sisters moved in (on St. Joseph's feast day as they had prayed for) but the bishop was still not cooperating. He came to visit the house and liked it, but gave no permission for Mass to be said there or for the Blessed Sacrament to be kept there. So, the sisters had no daily Mass again, and had to go out to a nearby church for Sunday Mass.

The bishop held back until April 18 when he finally gave permission. Four days later the convent was officially started.

In late May, as if Satan were making a last stand against Teresa, a terrible flood hit Burgos with the water reaching above the first floor windows and filling the rooms waist-high. The sisters wanted to leave, as neighbors were doing, but Teresa brought the Blessed Sacrament to the second floor and they all prayed before it the whole day long from 6 am to midnight.

Some time later she asked in prayer, "Lord, are you satisfied?" He answered, "Go, you must now suffer greater things still."

It was July and the house was established sufficiently that she could leave for Ávila again to resume her post as prioress. She never got there. She had to make a stop in Valladolid to get involved in some terrible family disputes over money. While visiting the Carmelite house she encouraged the sisters to pursue true holiness. Alas, the prioress treated her badly and as Teresa was leaving, she told the foundress, "Go and don't come back!" So much for loyalty!

At about this time she was quite ill, suffering "with her head, her throat, in all her bones." Since she had left Burgos, her mouth was often lined with blood, and she could hardly keep any food down.

Solving Problems

She stopped next at Medina del Campo, where some sisters were attempting to go beyond the Rule which limited Communion to Sundays and feast days. Teresa reminded them of the need for obedience and insisted they follow the Rule. This, despite their complaining they would die if they did not receive the Eucharist. She enforced the Rule, and they didn't die.

She received a visit from the Vicar Provincial who told her of trouble at the convent in Alba del Tormes and ordered her under obedience to go there. And so, despite feeling at the end of her strength, she detoured there next. After an extremely painful journey with hardly any food, she arrived on July 20, 1582. She was so tired that the prioress of that convent urged her to go to bed immediately, and she did.

She got up the next day and went about her business. That included scolding the woman supporting the convent financially for driving the sisters mad with her constant pestering. The woman agreed to change. Then, one of the Discalced priests from Salamanca came to tell her the prioress there had bought a new house which Teresa had forbidden. He told her it was too late to stop it since the papers had all been signed. She told him no, it was not too late and they would never have that house. She was right. The whole deal fell apart and never came to completion. She still had a bit of fight in her, despite being so sick!

Final Days

She continued on with her work until September 29, although she took more rest than usual each day. On the 29th she had a hemorrhage and went to the infirmary. On October 2 Teresa asked for the priest to come and hear her confession. The report got out that she would soon die.

On October 3 she requested viaticum, the final reception of holy Communion to strengthen her for departure from this world. When the priest arrived with the host, Teresa's face suddenly became radiant, young and beautiful. She got up and knelt down. Then, she began to sing as she had never sung before. The words included, "O my Lord and my Spouse, now the desired hour has come... for me to leave this exile..."

She gave thanks to God that she had been "a daughter of the Church," asked pardon of her sins from the sisters, and urged them to keep the Rule. At nine pm she received Anointing of the Sick. The next morning she turned on her side and continued completely still, in ecstasy for almost the whole day. At 9 pm she passed from this world. She appeared "gloriously young and beautiful." She was 67 years old. It was the feast of St. Francis of Assisi.

She was buried the next day. The date would have been October 5, but it became the 15th, since the Gregorian calendar took effect that day and 10 days were dropped from the calendar. This explains in part why her feast was, and is, celebrated on October 15th and not the 5th, which was the closest available day (after St. Francis' day) to her death.

Post Mortem

Nine months later Fr. Gracián came and they dug up her body. A great deal of moisture had entered the casket, but her body was incorrupt. From her casket a beautiful aroma filled the convent. In 1585 her body was taken to Ávila and many miracles occurred for those who touched it. A year later it was returned to Alba again.

She was beatified in 1614, and canonized in 1622, and named a Doctor (i.e., great teacher) of the Church–the first woman to be so honored–in 1970.

Gentle and kind though she was, Teresa was known for her witty, blunt sayings, including: "May God deliver us from stupid nuns!" (She admitted only sensible nuns.);"Where there is no obedience there are no nuns."; and "The bad inn [of life] lasts only a night." Always cheerful and funny, she would say "God deliver me from gloomy saints!"

At one point, after a very holy hermit, a woman, had died, Teresa compared her own penances to hers and wondered if she should not be doing more. When her confessor would not give her permission to do more, she considered disobeying him, so she could take on more such penances.

It didn't take long for the Lord to set her straight on the matter. Jesus appeared to her and commented, "No, daughter! The way you are following is the best... You know all the penances she practiced? I appreciate your obedience much more." From this it should be clear that being obedient is considered a great penance by the Lord.

She knew well the value of the Cross. She wrote, "When you embrace the Cross, you do not feel it" (that is, when you accept suffering for the love of God, it doesn't hurt so much anymore); "When you resolve to suffer the pain ceases." And, she knew the value of love over works: "...The Lord does not look so much to the grandeur of our works as to the love with which they are done." It seems certain that her works were grand because of her great love, for God, for the Church, and for her Carmelite brothers and sisters.

Reflection

Teresa of Ávila was one of the most active saints the Church has ever had. She founded 17 new convents for an Order she herself began (as a reform of the Carmelite Order) in the face of tremendous opposition. And, her first convent was not founded until she was 47 years old. She had only 20 years from that date until she died!

Despite all the troubles she had in founding convents–even in getting there amidst the cold or heat and often being sick–she was always cheerful and upbeat. Goodness knows she suffered great sorrows, especially when it seemed all her work would be wasted by having the Reform destroyed by the papal representative. Nonetheless, she always bounced back and trusted that the Lord would make things right. And He did!

Teresa showed us a beautiful example of obedience. She knew she could do nothing for the Lord without that virtue. And, she expected great obedience from her nuns as well.

One thing should be clear from her life (and from the lives of many other saints such as Ignatius of Loyola, John Bosco and Alphonsus Ligouri): If you are going to do important and great things for the Church, you will receive much opposition even from good people. It should remind us of the quote from Sirach:

My son, when you come to serve the LORD,
    prepare yourself for trials.
Be sincere of heart and steadfast,
    undisturbed in time of adversity.
Cling to him, forsake him not;

thus will your future be great.

Accept whatever befalls you,

in crushing misfortune be patient;

For in fire gold is tested,

and worthy men in the crucible of humiliation.

Trust God and he will help you;

make straight your ways and hope in him. (Sir. 2:1-6, NAB)

Teresa did indeed trust in God, and how blessed the world is that she did!

Sources

Auclair, Marcelle, *Saint Teresa of Ávila,* New York, NY: Pantheon Books Inc, 1953.

Teresa of Ávila, St., *The Collected Works of St. Teresa of Ávila,* Three Volumes, trans. by Keiran Kavanaugh and Otilio Rodriguez, Volume I (pp. 33-283); Volume III (pp. 85; 111-186; 217; 297-303), Washington, D.C.: ICS Publications, 1976.

Teresa of Ávila, St., *The Autobiography of St. Teresa of Ávila*, trans. by E. Allison Peers, Garden City, NY: Image Books, 1960.

Walsh, William Thomas, *St. Teresa of Ávila*, Rockford, IL: TAN Books, 1993.

Chapter Six

St. John Vianney
(The Curé of Ars)
(1786-1859)

Some saints start out as sinners and reform; others start out holy and get better. John Vianney was one of the latter. He was born on May 8, 1786, the fourth of six children born to Matthew Vianney, a farmer in Dardilly, France (not far from Lyons), and his devout wife, Marie Beluse. John had been consecrated to the Blessed Mother before his birth, something his mother did for all six children. His mother taught him from the earliest age to make the sign of the cross before meals. John learned that lesson well, such that one day, at fifteen months, when she forgot, he refused to start eating until it was done.

Youth

John was a lively boy, energetic at games, but determined to conquer his self-will so as to live the virtue of obedience. And, he was obedient, far more so than his brothers and sisters. When he was four, his younger sister decided she must have his rosary beads which he treasured. After some yelling and tugging, the boy sought justice from his mother. He got something better: detachment. She had him give the rosary to his sister, "for the love of the good Lord," but rewarded his generosity with a little statue of the Blessed Mother, something he had admired for a long time. "Oh! How I loved that statue," he proclaimed 70 years after, "Neither by day nor by night would I be parted from it... The Blessed Virgin was the object of my earliest affections."

When the bell for the Angelus rang at noon, John was the first to kneel for the prayers. He was often seen in a quiet place in the house on his knees praying before his precious little statue.

John's mother attended Mass every day. From the age of four John would beg to join her. He always praised his mother and gave her credit for his interest in prayer as a young boy.

At age seven John began to help shepherd the family flock of sheep and cows. During his break he would put his statue of Mary in a little shrine he made in the woods and there prayed the rosary. Occasionally he would arrange for his shepherd friend to cover for him while he went and prayed, at times for hours. When the nearby shepherd children asked about his devotion, he taught them the prayers–and virtue as well. Unfortunately, the other children knew little about the faith since the government had forbidden true Catholic worship in public, and their parents had not clung to the faith as had John's.

When one day a neighborhood girl suggested they might make a good couple, John shrank from the idea. "No, Marion," he answered, "Let's not even talk about this." Even at this young age he seemed to know his calling.

John's first communion had to be made in secret for fear of the government. Those who prepared him for this great event saw John as "a little saint." When his burning desire to receive the Eucharistic Lord was at last fulfilled, he seemed filled with joy. In fact, they had to rouse him from the room which served as a chapel when it was time to go. Years later his eyes filled with tears whenever he spoke of this event.

Priesthood?

At eighteen he began to feel strongly a call to the priesthood. His mother was delighted at the idea. When he told his father he got no response at all. This meant no. John was needed in the fields.

John obeyed his father, but prayed and hoped for nearly two more years. When a priest in the neighboring town, Fr. Charles Balley, began a small school for young men who felt called to the priesthood, John's mother pleaded with her husband to allow John to attend. His father gave in.

However, when John's mother and aunt approached Fr. Balley about John's studying with him, the priest turned them down. John's brother-in-law's attempt also failed, but he at least got the priest to speak to John. The young man's knowledge and love of the faith won Fr. Balley over. He accepted him.

John's troubles were not over; indeed they were just beginning. He struggled with Latin, even with the help of his (much younger) class-mates. Once, his tutor lost patience with John and hit him on the head before the whole group for his stupidity. John went down on his knees and begged the pardon of his twelve-year-old classmate. The boy was moved to tears by John's humility and embraced him. From that moment they became lifelong friends. His tutor, Matthias Loras eventually became the bishop of Dubuque, Iowa, and never forgot this event.

John couldn't seem to master his studies no matter how hard he prayed, fasted and worked. His landlady told Fr. Balley John was too weakened by his fasting and the priest spoke to his young student, "We must pray and do penance, but it is also a duty to eat and not ruin your health." He accepted the priest's advice and got the food he needed.

Nonetheless, he was still discouraged by his struggles with Latin and his other studies. He went to Fr. Balley and told him, "I want to go home." The wise priest saw John's discouragement and reminded him of the souls who needed saving. "Would you abandon them?"

This convinced John to stay, but he knew he needed help–a lot of help. So, he turned to God. He decided to go on a pilgrimage to beg God to help him get through this great trial. That summer (1806) John made a 60-mile Journey to the shrine of St. Francis Règis to pray for the grace to be able to succeed in theology, which was taught in Latin. He went on foot and begged his food from houses along the way. He arrived half-starved, but fulfilled his mission and made it home in one piece. Upon his return he began to make some real progress at last, much to the surprise of all.

The Army

However, in 1809 John was drafted into the army. This, it seems, was a mistake, since seminarians were to be exempt, but the mistake could not be corrected. He entered, but in two days became quite sick. He was hospitalized twice before receiving orders to report on January 5, 1810. Arriving early on his day to report, he made a visit to a nearby church. There he found consolation for his troubles, but by the time he finished praying and arrived at the military office it was shut down for the day. The next day he reported again at the office and was scolded for his tardiness. His unit had left without him, so they sent him out to catch up with them. Still weak from his illness, he couldn't travel fast enough to catch them.

Exhausted and feverish from his travels, he sat down to rest. There he prayed the rosary, asking Mary to help him. A young man popped up and offered him lodging for the night and he gladly accepted. When John discovered the man was a deserter, he was reluctant to stay with him but was too tired to argue. When he felt stronger he turned himself in to the mayor of the closest city. The mayor turned out to be a bit odd when it came to the laws of the military. He told the young man that trying to straighten things out with the army was hopeless, and offered him a hiding place!

He was taken in by the mayor's sister, who fixed him a place in the stable. He began to teach the children how to read and write, and of course, he taught them the faith. There were signals for John when the police came calling, so that he could hide. Once he had a close call when he had to hide beneath a pile of hay. The police actually began to poke around the hayloft with a sword and John felt the tip in his side. He was able to keep quiet, as he struggled to avoid suffocation beneath the hay.

He had been hiding for several months when a general amnesty was granted for deserters. John got the word in October that he was free to return home and resume his studies. It was with many tears and hugs that he left his friends at Les Robins and headed back to his family for a warm homecoming.

Home Again

It seems his unintended desertion was providential in his journey to the priesthood. Had he entered the army and stayed, his studies would have been put off a long time.

He returned home in January of 1811, just two weeks before his mother died. He would miss her deeply.

Studies

With mixed emotions John resumed his studies in Ecully after a 16-month delay. In late 1812 he was sent on to the minor seminary, where he struggled to learn philosophy in Latin. So, the professors decided to teach him and several others in French. In his own language, he began to learn, but slowly. John was older than all his classmates, and his teacher as well, but by now he was getting used to that. Though they didn't admire his learning skills, they admired his holiness.

In November, 1813 John moved on to study theology, in the Latin which had caused him such trouble. He again struggled with so little success that in just a few months he was told he could not continue.

John returned to Ecully to tell his sponsor, Fr. Balley, that he wanted to settle for being a brother. Fr. Balley wouldn't hear of it, and together they returned to the books. When time for the examination for priesthood arrived in May, Fr. Balley sent John. Alas, John was so nervous and so weak in Latin, he could hardly answer a question.

Despite his failure, because of John's devotion, and out of regard for Fr. Balley, the examiners did not fail John outright. They told him that if he could find a bishop in a different diocese to admit him they would not prevent it. This did not satisfy Fr. Balley. He went to Lyons to plead for his pupil. He persuaded them to test John back at his parish in Ecully.

There in a more relaxed setting, John was able to pass. Though he still didn't know Latin well, his name was submitted to the Cardinal's vicar-general, who was temporarily in charge of the diocese. The latter asked, "Is Vianney holy? Does he love Mary? Does he pray the rosary?" The enthusiastic "Yes!" of John's promoters brought victory. John would be ordained.

Priesthood at Last

On August 9, 1815, John-Marie Vianney was ordained a priest. He was 29 years old. There was one thing held back from the new priest: his faculties (i.e., permission) to hear confessions. So, the priest who would later spend three quarters of his life in the confessional, drawing penitents from all over the world, would be delayed several months from hearing his first confession.

No matter to John. He was at last a priest, and he understood as well as anyone the awesomeness of the priesthood. Years later he would say, "Oh! How great is the priest. He will only be understood in heaven. Were he understood on earth, people would die, not of fear but of love."

John's first assignment as a priest was to assist Fr. Balley, his mentor, at Ecully, much to the delight of both. There John continued to learn from his pastor, not only theology, but also the ways of prayer and penance. Both ate little and both competed to deny themselves comforts and to do penance.

John's preaching was said to be brief and clear, but poor at first. However, later when he preached great numbers came to hear him.

For more than two years John and his teacher carried out their priestly work in great harmony. Then, in December 1817, having suffered a painful ulcer on his leg for several months, Fr. Balley died at the age of 66. John had anointed his teacher and friend and given him viaticum (final holy Communion).

Another pastor was sent to Ecully, one far less devout than Fr. Balley. He saw John's penances as just too much, and he was disappointed that the young priest would not go with him to visit the rich parishioners or the other priests for social events. John claimed his cassock was too worn for social visits. So, the new pastor had John moved. He was sent to Ars, to be pastor of a nowhere parish of just 230 people, far from just about everything. It was well-known in the diocese that this sort of parish was given to priests from whom they expected little. He was told, "There is not much love for God in Ars; you will bring some into it." It was February 1818.

The Parish of Ars

John had some trouble finding Ars, but finally a shepherd boy told him the way. The young priest thanked him and said, "You have shown me the way to Ars; I will show you the way to heaven."

The young priest prayed before the Blessed Sacrament to seek guidance for the large task of converting his parish. He began to visit all his parishioners to discover those who had some faith, and those who did not. He set out right away to convert his parish by the most effective means possible: prayer and penance.

Long before dawn each day he went into the little church and lying face down on the floor prayed, "My God, grant me the conversion of my parish. I am willing to suffer all my life whatever you would lay upon me... only let my people be converted." He was seen in the woods once by a parishioner, praying this same prayer on his knees.

He had much of the furniture removed from his rectory, leaving only the bare minimum for his simple needs. His penances included sleeping on the attic floor with a log for a pillow; he ate very little, primarily just boiled potatoes. He would cook several potatoes and place them in a basket, taking out one or two when he was hungry. In his early years he often took on excessive penances, thereby harming his health, as he later admitted.

Though he was constantly contributing to the poor, and had virtually nothing for himself, he bought beautiful things for the church to give glory to God. He visited all his parishioners and discovered their lack of religious devotion was due to lack of knowledge. So, he set out to teach them all, young and old.

John always prayed a good deal before giving his catechism classes to the children. He rang the bell for the classes himself, led the opening prayers kneeling, and to stir them to listen, he would always begin with some moving thoughts, which often caused them to weep. He made sure they all had rosaries, providing many of them himself. His children became the best informed in the faith in the area.

His teaching of the adults took place during the Sunday sermon. For these, he began by bringing several books into the sacristy and reading a great deal about his subject. Then he spent time before the Blessed Sacrament, asking the Lord to guide him to speak the right words to reach his people. After this he would return to the sacristy to write as many as 30 to 40 pages. All this could take him up to seven hours. Then he began to practice giving the sermon by saying it aloud. This would bring him into the morning hours, with only an occasional nap–taken right there in the sacristy–to refresh him.

These sermons, unlike the ones he gave when newly ordained, would go on for an hour. He often spoke of heaven, and the need for conversion to get there. He preached strongly at times, even roughly, to the hardened hearts of his parishioners, often reminding them of hell.

He had little effect at first. In the spring the church was virtually empty on Sunday. The people would work in the fields on the Lord's day, after which they were off to the local tavern or out to dance the night away. John began to preach against the taverns, calling them "the devil's workshop, the school where hell sells its dogmas... where souls are battered, the place where families are broken up... where quarrels are started and murders committed." He was persistent in his attack, and eventually there were fewer and fewer tavern-goers. When one owner complained, saying he would lose his income, John gave him some money and convinced him to close. In time, the man began to live his faith to the full. Other taverns opened, but were no match for the young priest: they too were soon closed.

Fr. Vianney railed against cursing too, and gradually forced a reform in this area. For eight years he attacked Sunday work. He said in a sermon, "If we ask those who work on Sunday, 'What have you been doing?' they might answer, 'I have been selling my soul to the devil and crucifying our Lord... I am doomed to hell." He won this battle too.

Getting rid of the dancing addiction required a longer effort: 25 years. Dancing was an "attachment" for many in the town, and dances often degenerated into nights of sin. When the houses could not contain all the dancers, they moved to the stable, where the hay provided a bed for bad behavior. The holy priest could not ignore these things.

He cried out in his sermons, "Mothers may say, 'I keep an eye on my daughters.' You keep an eye on their dress; you cannot keep guard over their hearts. Go, you wicked parents, go down to hell where the wrath of God awaits you, because of your conduct, because you gave free rein to your children; go! It will not be long before they join you, seeing that you have shown the way so well..."

In addition to his stern, fatherly warnings in his sermons, he struck at the source of the problem. He met the fiddler on his way into town and offered to pay double his fee for him to leave without playing. The fiddler left satisfied.

He also preached against immodest dress.. This too took 25 years, but his persistence paid off. Modesty began to rule.

He encouraged those few who tended to be devout to form a group and pray the rosary after Sunday evening prayer. Thus he began what was to be called "The Guild of The Holy Rosary."

He was strict in the confessional. Those who refused to avoid the occasion of sin were denied absolution, sometimes for several years.

John started to renovate, enlarge and restore his little church, with the help of contributions from parishioners. His rectory was bare as could be, but the church had to be beautiful, and he was known to buy some very expensive furnishings for it. He wrote to the mayor at one point, "I want the entrance to the church to be very beautiful... for if the beauty of palaces of kings is increased by the magnificent approaches that lead up to them, how much more luxurious should be the approach to a church."

Opposition

His reforms were not always welcome. Some suggested his pale skin coloring was not to his penances—as was the case—but to a hidden life of sexual sins. They wove these lies into their foul street-songs. When an unmarried girl got pregnant, they tried to get people to believe it was his doing. Seven men in the parish who hated his reforms told him to his face he should leave Ars. His front door was pasted with human bodily waste, and for a year and a half a nasty person stood outside the rectory each night shouting insults. Slanderous letters were sent to his bishop, who sent another priest to investigate. (John was, of course, cleared).

Once, when John looked back on his life in that parish, he said, "If, on my arrival at Ars I had foreseen all that I would suffer there, I would have died on the spot." His response to his critics was to show them kindness and to encourage his friends to pray for them as he did.

Even his fellow priests were annoyed with him, and his success. They sent around a petition for all the priests to sign, accusing him of "sensationalism, ignorance, and [showy] poverty." When the petition came to him by mistake, he signed it, and sent it on to the diocese. His bishop once told a gathering of priests he wished they all had a touch of Vianney's "madness." By 1834 his fellow priests began coming to John for confession.

In 1841 John got a letter from a fellow priest, Abbé Borjon, age 32 (John was 54 at the time) which began, "Monsieur le Curé, when a man knows as little theology as you he ought never to enter a confessional..." He went on to insult John all sorts of ways. John wrote him back, saying,

How many reasons I have to love you my dear and honored co-worker. You are the only person who really knows me. Since you are so good and charitable to take an interest in my poor soul, help me to obtain the grace I have asked for so long–that of being replaced in a position I am unworthy to fulfill because of my ignorance–so that I may be able to retire into some corner, there to weep over my poor life... How much penance I must do, how may tears to shed!

Borjon got John's reply, walked to Ars where he "threw himself" at John's feet to ask forgiveness.

John prayed for a love of the many crosses he had to endure, especially the malicious rumors about his immorality, and his prayers were answered. He said, "To suffer lovingly is to suffer no longer... We should pray for a love of the cross. Then it will become sweet... Truly, there is no happiness but in the cross." At one point he said, "I thought a time would come when people would run me out of Ars with sticks, when the bishop would suspend me, and I should end my days in prison. I see, however, that I am not worthy of such a grace."

Eucharistic Devotion

Our saint began to rebuild the holiness in his parish by the best of ways: the Eucharist. He gradually guided "Mademoiselle d'Ars" to receive the sacraments more, especially Holy Communion. In a short time she began the practice of daily Mass. Her example drew some who had seldom been receiving the sacraments into daily Mass and frequent communion. With their pastor (who seemed to pray constantly before the Blessed Sacrament) as their example, more and more spent long periods in adoration before the tabernacle. One such man when asked what he did during his long visits there responded, "I just look at the good Lord and he looks at me." Fr. Vianney told this story often, and added, "Everything is in that, my children."

He breathed new life into the Guild of the Blessed Sacrament, which was all but dead when he arrived. He also brought new members into the Confraternity of the Rosary, welcoming men and young people for the first time. And, he began the archconfraternity of Our Lady of Victory, the only requirement of which was to pray one Hail Mary daily for the conversion of sinners. For this group he was able to enlist sixty men and young people. He also taught people to examine their conscience each day, and to read spiritual books.

John was often asked to lead missions at nearby churches, to which he generously agreed. On one mission, he had someone boil him some potatoes on the first night and never ate anything but those few potatoes for the whole week. Having preached—to congregations which wept at his words—and heard confessions long into the night all week, he would travel on foot sometimes six miles on a cold winter Saturday night to be back in his parish for Sunday.

Whenever a nearby parish was without a priest or the priest was older and not strong enough to do everything in his parish, John was ready to help. He would go in the evenings and visit the sick in some of these parishes two miles away or further. He helped out with baptisms, weddings and funerals as well. Once he visited a family who had asked for him in nearby Rancé. He walked through the rain and was soaked when he arrived. He was so sick with a fever that he had to lie down next to the sick man to hear his confession. He was sicker than the man he came to visit!

A School

John saw that there was a need for a school in Ars, since the only schooling children received was when a teacher was brought in for a while to instruct them. He began to save money for a girls school first, and then sent two of the most religious girls to a convent to study and prepare to run the school. He spent every penny he had plus many donations to buy a house for the new school. He opened the free school in 1824. Not only the local girls came, but those from other towns as well, and so they had to arrange a place for these out-of-town girls to live in the attic.

In 1827 he added a house, aptly called the Providence, for abandoned girls. In time they provided shelter for over sixty young women. Often they would be stretched to the limit in providing for their boarders. Once they were almost completely out of corn, and every source of help had been exhausted. So, John gathered together the remaining grains, placing them in a relic of St. Francis Regis. He invited his orphans to join him in praying devoutly for some sort of miracle. Then he sent the director to go see what corn was there in the bin. She went and found the storage attic so full of corn she could barely open the door! This was not the only time the prayers of the holy priest and his children for desperately needed food were answered with a miracle.

The Providence helped hundreds of children to get decent jobs and avoid evil. Though some left, many married well, others succeeded as maids, and some entered a convent. The holy pastor taught them religion every day himself. Initially this class was just for the children, but eventually flocks of pilgrims began to join them daily. In 1845 there were so many attending that they had to move these lessons to the church.

Transformation

Within 15 years of John's arrival, the parish was just about completely transformed. During the week the men would pray the rosary as they were working. When the bell rang for evening prayer, many came to the church to pray. Those who couldn't would often kneel in prayer in their own house. One woman walked through the fields and noticed that those working there used no foul language as was the custom in so many towns. When she complimented one farmer on this, he replied, "...it would be shameful to commit such sins when we live close to a saint."

Every hour the church bell would ring and those who could hear it would stop and say a Hail Mary. When it rang at 6 o'clock, am or pm, or noon, they would stop and say the Angelus. John would go out and visit the families in the evenings, and the people were happy to welcome him. Later, his almost constant hearing of confessions would put an end to these delightful visits.

Before Fr. Vianney came, people would hide the flaws in the products they sold: rottenness in their eggs, staleness in their butter, flaws in their cows. They felt no guilt stealing vegetables from other farms, nor did they concern themselves when their children came home with little stolen items. Under Fr. Vianney all that changed, and the people were very careful about avoiding such injustices. One mother discovered her son had brought home a pear he had taken from a fruit stand in town. She brought him back to the town and had him return the fruit with an apology.

The holy priest was always ready to go out and visit a sick parishioner. He was a father to them all and they loved him dearly.

There was one problem John was unable to solve for a long time: lateness for Sunday Mass. Each Sunday he sent his sacristan out to round up the people standing outside, but even so it was more than 30 years (!) before they were cured.

Sunday became a day of real quiet, for prayer and reflection, without any shops being open. They celebrated a number of feasts with considerable solemnity during the year, such as Corpus Christi, Sts. Peter and Paul and St. John the Baptist. The church would be filled for Mass in the morning and prayer in the evening on these days. He trained the altar servers himself and they were most inspiring in the way they carried out their duties. The banners and vestments were always remarkably beautiful.

A day famous for its solemnity at Ars was Corpus Christi, the feast of the Body and Blood of Christ. All could see how deeply John loved this feast of the Eucharist by the very way he would announce it. Dressed in magnificent vestments, he would carry the monstrance in procession with billowing censers, artillery blasts, bells, hymns, and two thousand in procession, many from nearby towns, giving glory to God. Our saint fixed his eyes on the Host, carrying the beautiful monstrance beneath a magnificent canopy. He prayed and wept tears of joy.

The "Grabber"

John's tireless work for the Lord drew the attention of the devil, who harassed the priest from 1824 on. The sounds of strong banging against the front door, yells and screams in front of the rectory, wagons seemingly rumbling through the rectory, furniture being overturned, the snarling and roaring of animals, and even a guttural voice calling out, "Vianney! Vianney! Potato eater!... I will get you!" were often heard by John in the middle of the night. Visitors too heard the noises. John came to realize that Satan was most active the night before some great sinner was to come and confess for the first time in many years. The priest was happy for the tip-off, if not for the frightening noises.

One morning as John was ready to leave the confessional for Mass, some parishioners told him that his room was on fire. He simply gave them his key, asking that they put it out, saying, "That villainous *grappin* ["little grabber"—the familiar nickname John gave to his opponent]! He could not catch the bird so he burns the cage!" Indeed, his bed was burned. The fire, which started by itself, it seems, became extinguished by itself, and it did not burn things nearby which logically should have been burned.

One night in 1827 Fr. Vianney was staying in a parish with some other priests for a mission and the devil made a terrible ruckus. When John explained the next morning that it was the *grappin*, the other priests told him it was his imagination. The next night the noises were even louder and hearing such a tremendous racket from his room they rushed there to discover him calmly lying in his bed which the demon had dragged to the middle of the room. He apologized for the noise but told them they could expect a "big fish"–a penitent confessing after decades of sin–for confession the next day. They still doubted it was the devil, but the next day, when a notorious sinner went to John for confession, they changed their minds. From then on, one of his greatest doubters believed John to be a saint.

In 1840 John encountered a woman apparently possessed by Satan. She proclaimed, "Oh how you wear me out... Ah, if only that Lady (Mary) would not protect you! ...Why do you preach so simply? You appear as an ignoramus. Why not preach in the grand style as they do in the towns? Ah, how those grand sermons delight me, which bother no one, which leave everyone to go their own way and do what they please!"

In 1850 Count Jules de Maubou attended a party where they called upon spirits and the table was lifted off the floor and their questions were answered by the table tapping the floor. This sort of entertainment was popular in Paris, as ouija boards are sometimes used today. Two days later he went to see his friend, Fr. Vianney, in Ars. When the priest saw his friend he immediately said to him, "Jules stop! The day before yesterday you had dealings with the devil. Come to confession!" He confessed his sin and promised to never dabble with such evil again.

In 1857 the archbishop of Avignon sent a priest and nun to bring a schoolteacher who was possessed by the devil to see John, hoping he could free her. The young woman tried to leave when they brought her in, saying there were too many people. John sent them all out and then had a heated conversation with her. After a short time of this, John freed her from the evil one, and she walked out the door calmly and gratefully. She went back to teaching full of joy.

A woman possessed by the devil once cried out to him: "How you make me suffer! If the world held three men like you, my kingdom would be destroyed. You have snatched more than 80 thousand souls from me." John told the woman's daughter to begin a novena to St. Philomena and bring her mother back the next day when he would hear her confession after Mass. The priest fulfilled his promise and by the time the woman had left Ars, she was back in the state of grace and free of her tormentor, the devil.

Fr. Vianney's reputation as a confessor spread far and wide. In 1827 people began to come from all over the neighboring area to ask for John's guidance. About twenty visitors came each day.

St. Philomena

After 1830 John began to introduce a devotion to St Philomena. Her tomb was just discovered in Rome about 1802, with the words *Pax tecum Filumena* (Peace to you Philomena) engraved on it. There was a broken glass vial which most likely contained her blood, presumably signifying that she was a martyr. The bones were the size of a fourteen-year-old girl. When her relics were moved to Mugnano in Naples, many miracles began to occur. Based on this, Gregory XVI authorized a feast day for her on September 9, which was only in 1961 removed from the calendar.

Although we have no historical data on her life, three people in various parts of the world had private revelations as to the details of her life. A sister in Naples gave the story that Philomena was a princess who suffered martyrdom at the hands of Diocletian because she would not marry him. It is most unusual to have only such information on a saint, and no real historical information.

Some time after 1830 John received a relic of St. Philomena, and began to attribute all the healings to her intercession. He would offer to pray for the person who was sick and then sent them to his little shrine of St. Philomena to ask her intercession. There were any number of cures. Through Fr. Vianney this newly discovered saint became famous throughout France.

More Confessions

From 1830 to 1845 the number of pilgrims coming to see or confess to the saintly priest increased yearly. By 1845 three or four hundred pilgrims arrived daily. By the year between 1858 and 1859, John's last, over 100,000 visitors came to Ars to pray and confess. There were not nearly enough hotels for all the pilgrims, so some stayed with the townspeople, while others slept in the meadows. Everyone had to wait their turn to confess, often a whole week, although occasionally he chose certain persons for immediate attention, knowing either that they were in a hurry or were wavering.

Once he sent someone out of the church to bring back a woman who had left because she could wait no more. Another time he pointed to a man whom he did not know, and who for many years had been away from confession. He invited him up and remarked to the man who was still mystified at being singled out, "It is a long time since you were at confession, no?" The man replied, "Something like 30 years." The priest corrected him, "It is 33 years. You were at such and such a place..." The man admitted John was right. "Ah well, so we are going to confession now, are we not?" The man could hardly say no. Once he agreed to confess he experienced "a sensation of indefinable comfort." The 20-minute confession changed the man's life. There were other similar cases of John hearing a person's confession after telling him how long it had been.

The holy priest would often weep over the sins people confessed. It was not uncommon for the penitent to leave the confessional in tears as well. One penitent asked him, "Why do you weep so much, Father?" John answered, "Ah, my friend, I weep because you do not weep enough."

John was extremely concerned for every soul, that it never be lost. He would say in his catechism classes, "What bitter grief to think that there are men who will die without loving God!" He would say from the pulpit some times, "Cursed by God! Cursed by God! What a misfortune! What a misfortune! And the people would weep, because John was weeping so.

John could be quite gentle with those who truly wanted to repent, but to those who did not, he could be equally firm. A woman from Paris was urged by her priest to stop at Ars on the way home from vacation, knowing she was leading a sinful life. As John was returning from a sick call he saw her in the street and said to this woman, who was a complete stranger, "Madame, please follow me." In private he told her what her sins were, at the end of which she asked him to hear her confession. He responded, "Your confession would be useless. I see two devils that enslave your soul, pride and impurity. I could only absolve you if you were to promise not to return to Paris. But, seeing your intentions, I know you will return there." He then told her she would fall into some terribly sinful ways.

She assured him she was incapable of such horrible sins, and proclaimed, "So I am damned!"

He replied, "I do not say that, but from now on, how hard it will be for you to save your soul!"

"What must I do," she asked.

"Come tomorrow and I will tell you," said the priest.

That night he prayed a long time and did great penances for this poor woman. The next morning he welcomed her ahead of others and told her, "You will leave Paris against your will to return to the [vacation] house you just came from. There, to save your soul, you must practice these penances..." and he told her the penances she must endure. She left without being absolved. She returned to Paris and saw she was about to fall into the horrible sins John had predicted, and she cried out for God's mercy and went off to her vacation house on the Mediterranean. She followed John's instructions despite her passion for sins of the flesh which she had indulged in for so long. In three months she was a new woman.

The refusal of absolution to this woman was the exception for John. He felt such compassion for those who had come from so far to confess. He told one priest, that in order not to discourage penitents, "I give them a small penance and perform the rest myself in their place."

The holy pastor converted many alcoholics. One woman thanked John since before her husband had gone to see him he would beat her more than speak kindly to her. After his visit he came home "meek as a lamb" and the beatings stopped. Another, after confessing to Fr. Vianney would walk a roundabout way to church so as not to walk near a bar and be tempted.

In Lyons a man who argued much with his wife over just about everything, left one day saying, "You'll never see me again!" On the street he saw a bus ready to leave for Ars, and on hearing there was a saintly priest there, he decided to get on the bus and go for a change in scenery. Once there he was deeply moved by the priest, and having heard him speak just twice, he returned humbly to his wife to begin a new life.

One atheist, an artist, on his way to a month-long vacation in Beaujolais met a friend on the bus who invited him to come with him to Ars to see a miracle-working priest. "I don't believe in miracles," was his reply. "Come," said his friend, and you will see *and* believe." The atheist decided to go to satisfy his curiosity. The next morning as John was on his way to say Mass, he noticed the man. After Mass he signaled him to go into the sacristy. Once there, he pointed to the confessional and invited the man to kneel there. He resisted, but then decided to humor the priest, but without any intention of changing his life. He told his story, and John, knowing he was not sorry, told him to go before the statue of St. Philomena and ask her to intercede for his conversion. "Come back tomorrow," the priest said.

He went, again out of curiosity, and stood before the statue. All of a sudden he was given the gift of faith and broke down weeping. He

ran out of the church pouring out tears of repentance. The next morning as he knelt before the priest, he blurted out, "Father, I don't
believe in anything... Help me!" He stayed another week and returned
to the faith, which he kept and spread for the rest of his life.

Guidance

Many came to John to ask if they should enter religious life. And
many were told to do so. One soldier asked, after serving John's
Mass, if he should enter a religious order. John replied, "Be sure you
do no such thing. The army needs an example like you."

John encouraged people to pray the rosary and especially to attend
daily Mass. He also encouraged praying the Angelus, and praying
with others. He said, "Private prayer resembles straw scattered here
and there over a field; if it is set on fire the flame is not powerful. But
if you gather those scattered straws into a bundle, the flame is bright
and rises in a soaring column toward the sky. Such is public prayer."
He would not permit people to fast when he saw they could not do
their work properly when fasting.

A woman who had a large family and was pregnant once again,
came to seek some encouragement from John. She was discouraged
and it showed. John picked her out of the crowd and commented,
"You look very sad, my child." She replied, "Well, Father, I am up in
years." He spoke to her kindly, "Take comfort, my child... If you only

knew the women who will go to hell because they did not bring into the world the children they should have! Do not worry over your burden; the Lord carries it with you. God does everything well. When he gives a young mother many children it's because he sees her as worthy. It is a mark of his confidence."

One day a priest asked John's advice on how to deal with his lazy parishioners. John said, "You have preached, you have prayed, but have you fasted?"

He spoke beautifully of the "food of the soul":

O my soul, how great thou art! God alone can satisfy you! The food of the soul, what is it but the body and blood of God! O beautiful food! God alone can be the food of the soul! God alone can suffice! God alone can fill her! God alone can satisfy her hunger! ...How happy are pure souls that unite themselves to God in Holy Communion!

One woman objected when John urged her to receive Communion more often. She said it was not customary to receive so often in her parish. John told her, "You have many friends. Choose the more virtuous among them and bring them to me; then you will no longer be alone." She returned with two others. John told them to receive more often as well, but he also wanted them to return in six months with "two or three others." After six months, twelve women came and all were to receive Communion more often.

Their pastor noticed the change and asked how it came about. Being told of the holy pastor of Ars, he went there to thank John for his efforts.

Daily Schedule

From the days of his service at Ecully, John would get up early–4 am–to pray before the Blessed Sacrament. At Ars he went even earlier, because as his biographer wrote, "the tabernacle attracted him irresistibly." What a magnificent attraction!

When the thousands of pilgrims began to come for confession, John would awaken at midnight or even before, to go over to church and begin his day. Before six am he left the confessional to say Mass. He would kneel for a time in adoration of Jesus in the tabernacle before offering the sacred mysteries which he loved so much to do. He took great pains to purchase the best vestments possible, and the most beautiful chalice. Though nothing was lowly enough for his poor rectory, nothing was too good for the Lord and the holy Mass! Some said John appeared as an angel when he said Mass. John would weep for joy during the whole time he was saying Mass. People were converted just seeing him say Mass.

After Mass John would kneel again motionless before the altar to make his thanksgiving. Then, back to the sacristy to bless religious objects and offer a few words of comfort to those in need. At about 8 am he drank a little milk in obedience to his bishop, after which he briefly visited his children at the Providence. Then, back to the confessional to hear the men, who had been waiting. At about ten he stopped and knelt motionless again on the stone floor to pray his breviary. One person described his eyes at this time as "bright and radiant." He was at peace with God. Then back to confessions until eleven when he gave a brief catechism teaching. Because of the huge crowds he had not time to prepare anything in advance, but the Holy Spirit seemed to have heard his prayer that he be able to speak without preparation.

Many people were moved to tears just to hear him teach his daily catechism. But John was the one who wept the most.

At noon John would lead the Angelus, after which he walked over to the rectory for lunch. Although it was just 30 feet from the church, it took him fifteen minutes to get there as he made his way slowly through the large number of people who stood along the path to the rectory. Many asked his prayers for healing or for the conversion of a spouse or child. In order to find room to enter the rectory he sometimes would throw a handful of medals to the crowd and while they were picking up these relics, he would slip inside alone.

Once inside his rectory he would take his little meal standing, while reading his mail. By 12:30 he was out again to visit the children at the Providence and then the sick. Two men would clear the way through the pilgrims who would often cut a piece of his cassock or even his hair as a souvenir relic.

A little girl from Lyons came and stood in the crowd in several places to get his blessing and receive a medal or crucifix which he might hand out to people. After three days of this, the priest handed her a medal and crucifix and commented, "Little one, that makes seventeen." She went back and counted. He was right.

In the afternoon he would go back to the church and kneel to pray his Divine Office again. He heard confessions of the women until five pm when he would stop to go to his rectory for just five minutes. Then, back to the church sacristy to hear the mens' confessions until about 8:00 pm. After praying night prayers he went back to the rectory for appointments. These finished, he locked himself in his room for more prayer and to read about the saints. Often he could barely climb the stairs, he was so exhausted. At last he fell into his hard bed for perhaps three hours of sleep, interrupted by coughing spells (several times an hour) and fevers.

A priest can become so involved in promoting Christ that he can forget to pray to Christ. This was not the case with Fr. Vianney. He was constantly getting back to his prayer from every activity he had to perform. He loved to pray and knew his need for it. He called it a "fragrant dew" and would say, "The more we pray, the more we love to pray." When he was deluged with penitents, he would choose an event in the life of Christ in the morning–the sorrowful mysteries were his favorites–and meditate on that all day long. One priest commented, "His life was one long prayer."

After so many pilgrims began to come, he was not able to go on retreat. When he went on his last retreat in 1835, the bishop sent him home, saying, "You don't need a retreat, whereas over there [in Ars] sinners want you."

His life of prayer kept him young at heart. He would say, "In a soul united to God it is always springtime." At times John would appear beaming with the joy of having God in his soul, but he knew he couldn't become attached to those consolations. He used to say, "When we have no consolations, we serve God for His own sake; when we have them, we run the risk of serving God for our own sake."

Even though he was so successful in saving souls at Ars, he always wished he could go and have time to pray to God alone and for a long time. He told a visiting religious, "I don't want to die a pastor, because I do not know of a saint who died in that position. I would like to have two years to weep over my poor life. Then, I would indeed love God!"

At one point he wrote to his bishop, "Monsignor, I am becoming more and more ill... I must spend parts of the night in a chair. I have attacks of dizziness in the confessional when I lose myself for two or three minutes at a time. Considering my sickness and age, I would like to leave Ars forever." He signed it "Vianney, a poor unfortunate priest." The bishop always ignored John's pleas, knowing how he was loved and needed in Ars. Some thought it was a temptation of the devil for him to want to leave a place where he was saving so many souls. He told a helper at the parish once, "The Lord gives me nearly all that I ask, except when I pray for myself."

Near Death

On May 3, 1843 the holy priest felt death approaching. He began the May devotions that year but all of a sudden he began to choke. A fever overcame him and they carried him to the rectory where the doctor soon arrived to diagnose his illness as pneumonia. He considered John just about ready to die. The pilgrims and the people of Ars were so disappointed to hear that the holy priest was dying. They all went to the church and prayed at the image of St. Philomena for his recovery.

The pilgrims insisted that someone bring their rosaries and medals for the dying priest to bless, which he was happy to do. On May 11 they anointed John, and rang the church-bell. John insisted on the bell because as he said, "A parish priest needs all the prayers he can get!" and the ringing of the bell signaled the end for the poor priest.

The doctor felt John's pulse and commented he had only thirty or forty minutes to live. John then turned to the Blessed Virgin Mary and his patroness, St. Philomena, to say, "Ah! If I can still be of use in saving a few souls..." The moment he said this, he started to improve. He opened his eyes and was able to speak again. Then a fever came over him. The people by his bedside didn't realize he had taken a turn for the better. They were hoping he would last through the night.

New Life

The next morning after a special Mass was celebrated for him at the altar of St. Philomena, his fever left him and he rested calmly. Then, he declared, "I am cured!" Indeed he was cured; his strength soon returned and he was able to say Mass. The doctors, however, forbade him to hear confessions for some weeks and John obeyed. He would have 16 more years to serve his people.

Once the doctor permitted him to hear confessions, John went back to work immediately–at 1:00 am! The doctor insisted, however, that John eat two meals a day until he was back to full health. For lunch he was to eat a little meat and a quarter glass of wine. The bishop concurred with the doctor's orders and John obeyed, but he felt bad about it. "I have become a glutton!" he would say, and his listeners would smile at his exaggeration.

In September John was given permission for a much needed vacation. It would be his first. He went to stay with his brother at Dardilly, a seven-hour walk from Ars. John was so exhausted when he arrived that he had to get into bed right away. That was September

12, 1843. By September 15 word had gotten around at Ars that Fr. Vianney was now in Dardilly, and so the pilgrims went there hoping to confess to him there. And, they were not disappointed. He went into the confessional at the parish there and began to hear their confessions.

On September 16 a priest arrived with a letter from the bishop, responding to John's request for an easier assignment after his illness. He offered John the position of chaplain at a small parish in Beaumont. He asked John, however, to consider it carefully with much prayer before accepting. So, on September 18 John set out for Beaumont. After saying Mass there and serving the Mass of Fr. Raymond, his former assistant, he decided not to stay, but to return to Ars. Back he went, and the people greeted him with great joy. He told them, "I shall never leave you again, my children." The pilgrims had stopped coming, so John had a few days' rest before word got out that he was back and the throngs began coming from all over.

In 1849 John began to raise money to pay for missions–several days of talks, Masses, and confessions by visiting priests in various parishes. He would receive 5,000 francs here, 6,000 there for missions in poor parishes that could not afford the 3,000 it cost to pay for a mission. People heard about his enterprise and gave him hundreds of thousands of francs to help. Every penny he could find he spent on this effective means of spreading and strengthening the faith.

In September, 1850 two of the children of the La Salette (France) appearances of our Lady came to visit the holy priest. John had already heard of the 1846 events there when in 1847 pilgrims returning from La Salette stopped at Ars to mention it to him.

Many pilgrims were healed through the intercession of the holy Curé and his dear St. Philomena, but the stories of those who were not healed provide deep insights into God's ways. A poor young girl, François Lebeau, asked healing of her blindness. The priest told her, "My child, you can be cured, but if God restores your sight, your salvation will be less assured; if you consent to your affliction you will go to heaven, and I even guarantee you will have a high place there." The girl saw the truth of what he said, and completely resigned herself to her blindness, never again asking for a cure.

In another case, that of Claudine Vinet, the Curé won the healing of her blindness and deafness, but warned her, "You will become deaf for another twelve years. It is God's will!" It happened just as he foretold: she lost her hearing again but twelve years later it was restored.

The saint seemed also to be given knowledge of the whereabouts of departed souls. A widow who had lost her husband to suicide went to pray at Ars. She was in line awaiting confession when the priest, who had never seen her before walked by and stopped before her. He said to her, "He is saved! He is in purgatory... Between the bridge and the water he had time to make an act of contrition. Our Blessed Lady obtained that grace for him... Though he had no religion he sometimes prayed the Marian prayers with you in May. This merited him the grace of repentance..." O how Mary repays even a small tribute made to her!

One brief incident shows our saint's intimacy with God. A devout woman once reached for his hand to kiss it, but he pulled back saying graciously, "Oh! Do not rob me of my ring!" She looked and saw a wedding ring on his left hand, something no one had ever seen before. It is believed that this ring, never visible again, was a sign of his spiritual marriage with God, a great privilege shared by such saints as St. Catherine of Siena, St. John the Almoner, St. Lawrence Justinian, Bl. Henry Suso, St Margaret of Cortona and St. Teresa of Avila.

Final Days

John began to weaken greatly in 1859. On Corpus Christi he was too weak to carry the monstrance in procession. In July a holy woman came for her last visit to confess to him. As he bid her farewell, he said, "We shall see each other in three weeks!" She thought this odd since she had no intention to return. But, in three weeks they would both be dead, reunited in the Kingdom.

The end of July that year brought blazing heat. The air was so hot and humid it made breathing difficult, and inside the church it was stifling. On July 29, the holy pastor went to his church at 1:00 a.m. as usual. Immediately he felt as if he were being smothered with the heat so that he could scarcely breathe, and he repeatedly had to go outside for air. He had a burning fever as well. He went to bed, announcing, "It is my poor end. Call my confessor."

His confessor came and the saint made his last confession in peace. On August 2 he received Viaticum and anointing. On August 4, 1859, at 2:00 a.m., John Vianney breathed his last. He was seventy-three.

On May 31, 1925, two weeks after another French saint, St. Thé-rèse of Lisieux, John Vianney was canonized a saint. He is the patron saint of parish priests.

Reflection

The call to priesthood is a mysterious thing. John Vianney felt that call from a young age, but faced an uphill battle to fulfill it. He struggled and struggled, despite his inability to learn Latin, to complete his studies. His refusal to give up and his devotion to the rosary carried him through. What he lacked in intelligence, he made up through prayer.

His first pastor was a great friend and example, but his second wasn't holy enough to appreciate this eager priest, so he had him transferred. John was sent to the farthest edge of the diocese, a place where there was little love for God. He had no plan but God's plan, so he obediently went.

Again, he struggled, not with Latin this time, but with his stubborn parishioners who didn't want to change. But armed with his hours of prayer before the Blessed Sacrament, he was stronger than his opponents. Little by little the people became holy.

As he began to succeed and people took notice, the priests became jealous, and criticized him to the bishop. What pain that must have cost John–the scorn of his own brother priests–even though the bishop was not fooled by their petty criticisms. The holy priest had prayed to love the cross (a healthy thing to do!), and this rejection by his peers would be part of his cross. The devil too, tried to discourage him, but John made light of that as well. All of this should serve as a reminder to us that holiness and suffering go together. But, as we saw in John, the suffering doesn't snuff out joy or happiness.

What an example for priests and laity alike: his love for the Mass; his love for prayer before the Eucharist; his love for the Rosary; his love for the poor; his establishing an orphanage; his providing beautiful things for the church and altar, while living in poverty himself; and, of course, his unending commitment to the sacrament of Penance and Reconciliation. These are the things that will make us holy... and that made John Vianney a saint.

Sources

Monnin, Alfred, *The Curé of Ars*, translated by Bertram Wolferstam, S. J., (Identified as "M" in paragraph references), St. Louis, MO: Herder Book Co., 1924, pp. 20, 38, 65-68, 199-207.

Thurston, Herbert J., S. J., and Attwater, Donald, *Butler's Lives of the Saints*, Volume III, Westminster, MD: Christian Classics, 1981, p. 283.

Trochu, Abbé Francis, *The Curé d'Ars* (Identified as "T" in paragraph references), Rockford, IL: Tan Books and Publishers, 1977, pp. 5-67; 80-149; 171-262; 279-375; 425; 521; 540; 545; 554-558 .

Rutler, George, *The Curé d'Ars Today*, San Francisco: Ignatius Press, 1988, pp. 69, 144, 184, 185.

Web site, http://www.philomena.us/main.asp, on St. Philomena.